ANTIQUE TRADER'S
COMPREHENSIVE GUIDE TO

AMERICAN PAINTED

Porcelain

WITH VALUES

by Dorothy Kamm

FOREWORD BY
RALPH AND TERRY KOVEL

ANTIQUE TRADER BOOKS

A Division of Landmark Specialty Publications
Norfolk, Virginia

Dedication

To my grandfather Joseph Kampf, whose gifts of china piqued my interest in this artform, who always encouraged my interests, and who took pride in my accomplishments.

He experienced life in the late Victorian era, showing an appreciation for the finely made and artistically decorated, whether a piece of furniture, an article of clothing, tableware, or a decorative item, a legacy he passed onto me.

Copyright 1999 by Dorothy Kamm

All rights reserved. No part of this publication may be reproduced, stored in a retrieval system, or transmitted in any form or by any means, electronic, mechanical, photocopying, recording, or otherwise, without prior permission in writing from the publisher.

Trademarks and copyright of products listed in this book are the sole property of their respective trademark and copyright owners. Copyrights for items depicted in photographs and illustrations are reserved by their respective owners, and the items are depicted here for the sole purpose of identification. The content of this book is the work of the author, and is not authorized, approved, or endorsed by any manufacturer, licensee, or trademark or copyright owner listed herein. This book is published without warranty, solely for the educational and informational benefit of the reader. None of the information, advice, or pricing data presented is guaranteed in any way.

Cover, left to right: Teapot, signed "C.E. Tolehard, 1914", part of a four-piece tea set, $225-275; Salt dip, signed "Tossy", ca. 1892-1907, part of set of six, $60-90; cake plate, ca. 1902, $45-55; creamer, signed "G Sitz", ca. 1904-1938, $15-25; candlestick, ca. 1900-1915, part of four-piece dresser set, $150-225; vase, signed "E. Sprecht", ca. 1880s, $35-55.

ISBN: 1-58221-008-X
Library-of-Congress Catalog Card Number: 99-61636

Editor: Tony Lillis
Graphic Designer: Kevin Gilbert
Copy Editor: Sandra Holcombe
Assistant Editor: Wendy Chia-Klesch
Cover Design: Heather Ealey
Production Assistant: Marshall McClure
Photographer: Dorothy Kamm

Printed in the United States of America

To order additional copies of this book, or to obtain a catalog, please contact:
Antique Trader Books
P.O. Box 1050
Dubuque, Iowa 52004
1-800-334-7165
www.collect.com

Table of Contents

Foreword 5
Acknowledgments 7
Introduction 9
Styles and Movements 13
Decorative Techniques 16

Chapter 1. The History of the American China Painting Movement . . .21

Chapter 2. Lasting Impressions: The Front Hall 27
    The Custom of Calling .27
    Card Trays 28

Chapter 3. Socializing with Society: The Parlor 31
    Whatnots: The Pride of the Parlor 32
    Foot Fetish 36
    Overdone Overmantels 37
    Green Dreams 38
    At Your Service 39
    Afternoon Receptions .40
    Tea Time 45
    Five O'Clock Tea 52
    Hot Chocolate 56
    Silhouettes and Spouts 58
    Lemonade 61
    Packing Punch 61
    Parlors and the Pleasures of Idleness vs. Living Rooms 63

Chapter 4. Dealing with Decoration: The Dining Room 65
    A Matter of Course 70
    Beer Basics 72
    At Your Service 76
    Plates for Service, Plates for Display 77

Chapter 5. Condiments and Compliments: Food Flavorings 89
    Spun, Nipped, or Spooned, Sugar Has Remained the Choice Sweetener . . .89
    Worth Its Salt 93
    Buttering Up 98
    Mustard Pots and Mayonnaise 103
    Cruets 108

Chapter 6. Breakfast and Lunch 111
    Beginning with Breakfast 111
    Sticky Sweeteners: Maple Syrup 115
    Lunch Bunch 116
    Tutti Frutti 119
    To Serve or Not to Serve: Claret and Grape Juice 123
    The Setting 124
    Card Parties 125

Chapter 7. The Dinner Party . . . . **.127**

Party Time 127

In the Beginning 128

Contained Within 131

Served with Relish 132

Pressed for Service 136

Pile on the Protein 137

To the Nines 139

Ramekins: Dating by Shape and by Decoration 141

Just Desserts 143

Cultivating Coffee and Culture 146

Closing Time 150

Ambiance is Everything 151

Is Your Antique Dinnerware Dangerous? 151

The Future of China Painting Products 152

Chapter 8. Male Order: The Library . . . . **.155**

Up in Smoke 155

Liquor License 158

Downsizing 159

Chapter 9. Feminine Retreat: The Bedroom and Boudoir . . . . **.161**

Chambersticks and Candlesticks 162

Dressed for Success 163

Hair Receivers and Hair Art 167

Hatpins, Stickpins, and Incense Burners 169

Collar Button Boxes 170

Shaving Mugs 170

No Time for Contemplation 171

Appendix. Ascertaining the Functions of Antique China:
Resources and References . . . . **.172**

Museums 173

Historical Homes 176

Historical Societies 177

Glossary 178

Selected Bibliography 182

Abbreviations 187

Alphabetical Listing of Artists and Studios 188

Index 190

About the Author 191

Foreword

Years ago we thought it would be fun to try our hands at china painting. We bought the plain white dinner plate, the proper paints, several thin brushes, and we started. The idea was good; the result was terrible. We discovered it takes artistic talent to create a shaded rose or an attractive group of fruits. So when we looked at our collection of nineteenth century English porcelains, we wondered how pieces that required so much labor and talent could be sold for comparatively little money. The first of the hand-painted china pieces in the United States came soon after the 1876 Philadelphia Centennial Exposition, and soon china painting was a pastime of thousands of wives and daughters. How, we wondered, did the woman of limited training create painted china of surprisingly good quality? Why, we wondered, did the hobby of china painting almost disappear after 1915?

Dorothy Kamm has written this book to explain it all. She includes history and pictures of the best examples of painted porcelain. She tells how designs were distributed and how techniques of painting were learned. The book is also a history of food service in America, explaining the form and use of the mustard pot, celery dish, lemonade pitcher, salt dip, and more. She also tells how the flowers, the colors, and the style of the painting help date it. If you collect hand-painted china, or if you want to create new examples in the old style, you will find this book authoritative and thorough, attractive and readable. It has the touch of the expert.

Ralph and Terry Kovel

Acknowledgments

There are many people involved in the writing and publishing of a book, providing encouragement, information, and assistance. To begin with, I must acknowledge Judy Ladd for recommending that I write another book on American painted porcelain. Without her suggestion, I would not have considered undertaking this project.

Once again, I thank my husband Dean Cohen and my daughters Erica and Julia for their patience, accompanying me while I shopped for antiques, indulging my creative streak, and respecting my work. I wish to acknowledge the unceasing encouragement and love from my parents Blanche and Irving Kampf, and my in-laws Miriam and Bernard Cohen.

I am indebted to my china painting students Elizabeth Cusato, Jean Jemmott, Judy Ladd, Diane Marcks, and Earleen Rowell for the forum they gave me when I read my manuscript during class; Dr. Dean S. Cohen, Dr. Shirley Dunbar, and Dr. James D. Henderson, Jr., for their invaluable observations, comments, and editorial suggestions; Dr. James D. and Marge Henderson, Jr., for their hospitality and book loans; Richard Rendall, for providing me with a copy of Mary Louise McLaughlin's book, and for his insights; Tim Ingram, for sharing his knowledge, copies of his *Keramic Studio* magazines, and Thayer and Chandler catalogs; Kyle Husfloen, for informing me about the archives at Sinsinawa Mound; Garrett Smith for sharing his references; William B. Wright, for his encouragement; Jessica Kole and Chris Elam, for accompanying me on antique expeditions; Chris Elam and Shelley Camilli for their gifts of porcelain; and to the numerous good people on the Treasure Coast who have rallied around me. I am grateful to my editor Tony Lillis for his support and encouragement, and for posing challenging questions that sparked the development of important ideas and topics, strengthening my manuscript.

I am indebted to the librarians of the St. Lucie County Public Library system; the Milwaukee County Public Library, downtown facility; Susan Summerfield, among others, at the Newberry Library; and Linda Naru and Tolisa Mitchell at the Center for Research Libraries in Chicago. I would also like to acknowledge the following individuals and organizations for sharing their research and expertise: Anne B. Shepherd, Reference Librarian, Cincinnati Museum Center; Anita J. Ellis, Curator of Decorative Arts, Cincinnati Art Museum; Judith Austin, Coordinator of Publications, Idaho State Historical Society; Dr. James D. Henderson; Rose Kanusky; Ralph and Terry Kovel (and for writing the Foreword); Jon Rarick, President, TransWorld Supplies; and Sandra Spence, Executive Director, Society of Glass and Ceramic Decorators.

I am grateful to Mr. and Mrs. James G. Bowden III, Roberta Deemer, Dr. Shirley Dunbar, Dr. James D. Henderson, Rosemarie Kanusky, Sue Phalen, Richard Rendall, Anne Wilder, and Mary Ann Gans of A Certain Ambiance Antiques in Stuart, Florida, for allowing me to photograph their porcelains. I also thank Carolyn Bowler of the Idaho State Historical Society and John Powell of the Newberry Library in Chicago for providing pictures.

Without the generosity of these people, this book would not have been successful. I thank all of you, and any others whom I may have inadvertently excluded.

Dorothy Kamm
June 1999

Introduction

The porcelain sitting on shelves and tables in antique shops and shows, and as heirlooms in homes, have stories to tell of a bygone era. Between 1877 and 1917, tens of thousands of American porcelain artists produced millions of hand-painted wares, many of which survive today. This book's purpose is to expose the reader to a past era quite distinct from our own, and share the integral role that porcelain wares played in everyday life in the last quarter of the nineteenth century, and first quarter of the twentieth.

Have you ever been baffled trying to correctly identify the function of a piece of porcelain? For those who collect or have inherited antique china, identifying the functions of objects poses a variety of challenges. Many objects considered essential and taken for granted in a particular time period, became obsolete due to technical advances and societal changes. Other china objects were pieces designed for specialty items of the time, such as celery, condensed milk, and canned sardines. Then, too, the function of a piece of porcelain may have changed over time, adapted to fulfill a new purpose. Unfortunately, much of this type of information has been lost because people did not chronicle their everyday lives. Most people grow up taking for granted the china our grandparents and great-grandparents used on special occasions, as well as on a daily basis.

I wondered about the functions of American painted porcelain the first time I purchased a double-handled, 14-inch long oblong tray decorated with various nuts. What did its long shape and its decoration tell me about its intended function?

Back then, my research had focused on the history of porcelain production and the American china painting movement. After examining every book and periodical in the Art Institute of Chicago's Ryerson Library, as well as in my local county library system, I still felt that my knowledge was incomplete, including the intended use of my tray. There were too many questions that remained unanswered.

I began broadening my search to include books on period interiors to obtain a more thorough understanding of how these porcelains related to the culture and setting of the time period. One book in particular, *Recreating the Historic House Interior* by William Seale (Nashville: American Association for State and Local History, 1979) proved to be a bonanza, for it instructed readers how to research a period home and the decorative objects it once contained. I was able to adapt Seale's research method to American painted porcelain. My search expanded to encompass references on dining habits and etiquette, old china catalogs and periodicals. I finally found the alternate route to the dead end I had faced when my research scope was limited.

Later on, while perusing old china catalogs, I discovered that my oblong tray was listed as a sandwich tray. Perhaps this tray was part of a tableware set that included nut bowls. Perhaps a sandwich made from date nut bread was served on it. It's even possible that the decoration was just that—decoration—and had nothing to do with its function, similar to the intriguing fact that rarely were lemonade pitchers decorated with paintings of lemons! My quest for answers about other pieces of porcelain continues.

Beyond appreciating American painted porcelain for its artistic beauty, a whole new world of excitement awaits the collector who understands how these pieces were used, and the circumstances that lead to their creation. Through inspection of their physical characteristics, i.e., their shape, size, and decoration, combined with resources that will be elucidated in this text, one can analyze and apply the information revealed in the research process and draw conclusions.

Hair receivers, for example, were part of every dresser set in the late Victorian era in America defined by historians as the period between 1876 and 1915, but why did anyone even want to collect loose hair strands? One must know about the sociology and the artistry of that time period to find the answer. Victorians possessed sentimental attitudes towards their friends and families, and would weave elaborate pictures and jewelry out of their loved one's hair as a remembrance. This activity was done as much out of love as of leisure.

In the same vein, china painting was one activity that many pursued at this time. People put into practice the ideal of the Aesthetic Movement that strove to turn common objects into works of art. This movement started in England in the mid-nineteenth century, and arrived in America at the 1876 Centennial Exposition held in Philadelphia. It exerted its influence until around 1890.

As we approach the new millennium, we now have the perspective to appreciate and understand these forgotten treasures. Chapter one provides the historical information germane to understanding the china painting movement and the objects that were decorated within the context of the time period in which they were created.

In this book we will tour an average middle class Victorian home. Room by room, porcelain and customs relating to its use will be covered in depth. Porcelains from the 1920s, 1930s, and 1940s also are included to illustrate the evolution—or stasis—of objects and their design. Through easy-to-follow formats, the following chapters will analyze and identify common objects and their places within each setting.

But by no means is the purpose of this book to depict and discuss every type of porcelain item that was ever manufactured. That would be an impossible task. Some of the pieces discussed at length are common, while others are more obscure. This gives the reader a good start on his or her quest to identify porcelain treasures and formulate an understanding of their evolution.

All pictures feature porcelains painted by American artists, despite the markings of foreign factories. Monetary values reflect condition, rarity of an object and of design, and artistic excellence. Size, too, may or may not factor in pricing. For example, a 9-inch diameter punch bowl may be worth around $400, while the value of a slightly larger, 11-inch diameter punch bowl may be worth double that amount, or more. Age does not yet bear a marked influence in pricing this category of hand-painted porcelain. Market driven trends, such as collector clubs, or the popularity of a particular style, create market demand, which in turn, affects pricing.

Pairs and sets tend to cost less than each individual piece that comprise a set. This is the American way of thinking, i.e., giving a discount for buying in bulk. Additionally, it is more difficult to sell a set, rather than an individual item. Most buyers are interested in only certain types of porcelain, such as cups and saucers, and they have spending limits. Sets also require more thought regarding storage and display.

Prices represent realistic, average, retail ranges. The date of manufacture is provided when the painting is undated, or approximated based on painting subject, style, and color palette when a factory backstamp is lacking. Although limited information exists, studios and artists are identified with location and dates whenever possible.

The detective work involved in unraveling an object's origins is part of the process of collecting. How and why forms developed was dependent upon existing models fashioned in other materials, as well as practicalities. Necessity being the mother of invention, craftspeople and artisans developed new forms and improved upon existing ones to provide better service.

But where does one turn to find information that will help unravel the sometimes confusing process of porcelain identification and appraisal? This book represents the start of a journey, delving into our Victorian past, and providing the tools that will make one's quest successful. For the serious researcher, the latter part of this book will assist you in uncovering the functions of antique china. Listed are the resources and references which can be employed, as well as the museums, historical homes, and historical societies where American painted porcelain can be viewed. Time spent examining books, investigating old magazines and catalogs, and visiting historical homes and museums, will further provide a greater understanding of not only how our ancestors lived, but how they used their household porcelain.

Author's Note: *Our language has changed during the past one hundred years. Many words that were hyphenated are now one word. For others, their spellings were the same as British English, or use French vowels. This can be confusing to contemporary readers, who may think a word is misspelled. For purposes of accuracy, old-fashioned word spellings are used in quoted items as they originally appeared in print. Items are identified by terms used in period china catalogs.*

Mrs. R. E. Halleck, Boise, Idaho, ca. 1890s. (Photo credit: Idaho State Historical Society, 387/B)

"IT IS LARGELY DUE TO THAT EARLY CRAZE FOR 'CHINA PAINTING'
THAT ART HAS BEEN BROUGHT INTO THE LIFE OF THE PEOPLE IN
THIS COUNTRY, FOR THE FINE ARTS WERE AND ARE LARGELY
CONFINED TO A SPECIAL CLASS, WHO OCCUPY A NICHE OF THEIR
OWN AND SPEAK A SPECIAL LANGUAGE. TO TAKE TO PICTORIAL ART
IS ALMOST LIKE GOING INTO A CONVENT AND RENOUNCING THE
OUTER WORLD, WHILE THE DECORATIVE ARTS ARE BY THE PEOPLE
AND FOR THE PEOPLE AND FLOURISH BEST AS PART OF THE LIFE OF
THE PEOPLE. THEY ARE IRON IN THE BLOOD AND BREATH IN THE
LUNGS. THEY CREATE AN UNCONSCIOUS ATMOSPHERE IN WHICH
WE LIVE AND MOVE AND HAVE OUR BEING."

"Looking Backward"
Henrietta B. Paist, Keramic Studio, *July–August 1918*

Styles and Movements

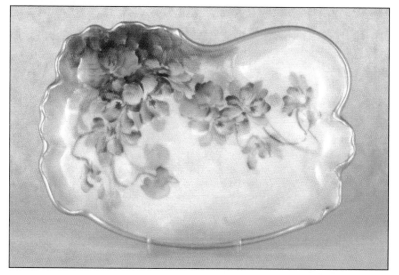

1875-1890
Aesthetic Movement

Naturalism reigned in porcelain paintings, and subjects were depicted in a realistic style that recorded natural quirks. Violets, roses, and sunflowers were rendered in jewel tones of rich purples, rubies, and saturated yellows. Fruits depicted on porcelains were portrayed in an autumnal palette of russets, ochers, maroons, and warm greens. (The Renaissance Revival style [1865-1885], which overlapped this movement, shared in common color palette and subject matter.)

1880s-1890s
French Style

This style employed gilded rococo curves and scrolls. Pastels, such as pale blue, ivory, light warm and cool greens, and soft pinks were used for delicate floral renderings.

1875-1890s
Anglo-Japanese Style

The craze for things Japanese was interpreted in porcelain painting in a variety of ways. Designs could be asymmetrical and simple, rendered in soft, neutral hues, or bold and graphic, utilizing complementary color palettes. Favored motifs included birds on branches, cherry blossoms, fans, and textile-inspired medallions or crests.

1880s–1890s
Royal Worcester Style

A style of decoration created by England's Royal Worcester porcelain factory and influenced by Japanese Satsuma wares. Characterized by matt ivory-tinted grounds and pastel-colored flowers that oftentimes had gilded outlines.

1880s–1900
Exotic Revival

Motifs were based on abstract patterns from foreign cultures documented by Owen Jones. Intricate Islamic patterns were particularly emulated. It was during this time that conventional, i.e., geometric, designs developed in porcelain decoration.

1890s–1920s
Arts and Crafts Movement

Conventional-style designs, which could be abstract interpretations of floral motifs or simply geometric compositions, were executed in flat or slightly modulated hues. Earth tones of olive and moss green, ocher, terra cotta, maroon, and brown predominated. Matt finishes were favored.

1890–1915
Art Nouveau Style

Swirling patterns of stylized flowers, birds, and fruits were rendered in muted tones of green, lilac, and purple, as well as olive green, sage, and mustard.

1900-1920 Colonial Revival Style

During this time the trend for white and pastels, particularly pale blue and yellow, replaced the more brilliant hues of the previous century. Backgrounds were toned down with soft hues. Iridescence also became vogue, particularly mother-of-pearl luster.

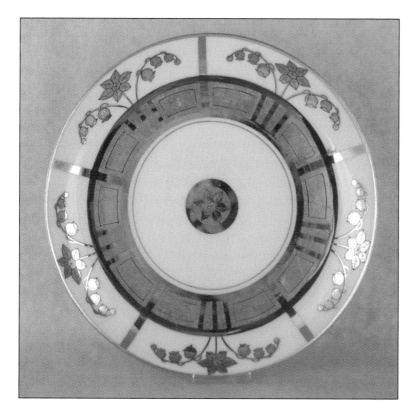

1915-1930s
Art Deco Style

Shiny silver was contrasted with burnished gold in geometric patterns, often emphasized by black outlines and backgrounds. Metallic tones were combined with burnt orange, pale blues, greens, and yellows. The use of iridescent lusters in porcelain decoration frequently appeared.

Decorative Techniques

The application of the various types of decorative mediums onto glazed porcelain surfaces all required kiln firing at over 1,350 degrees Fahrenheit to mature the materials and to make them permanent.

The nasturtiums and ground color were painted with overglaze paints, which also were called mineral colors.

The dark blue panels on this bowl are covered with matt paint, the light blue with overglaze paint. Butterfly wings are mother-of-pearl luster. Border bands are burnished gold.

Overglaze paints: Paints, which were derived from metallic salts combined with flux, applied over a glazed porcelain surface. Characterized by a soft sheen.

Matt paints: Paints derived from metallic salts but lacking flux, which created a dull, velvet-like, and opaque surface.

Lusters: Metallic salts that produced an iridescent surface when heated in a kiln.

Gilding: The application of various golds. Bright gold had a high shine. Roman gold was burnished to a soft sheen. Green gold was created by adding silver and oxide of chrome. Red gold had additional red oxide of iron and purple of cassius added to the gold powder base. Burnished bronzes were deeper in color than gold. Like gold, bronze finishes were available in various colors, such as green bronze, yellow bronze, and red bronze.

The turquoise "jewels" dotting the rim and foot of this of the salt dip were created from tinted enamel.

The flowers and border motifs on this jardiniere are filled with multicolored enamels.

The scrolled, latticed, and dotted border was applied with raised paste, which was then covered by burnished gold.

Enamels and Raised Paste: Pastes were used to create dimensional effects. Enamels were white or tinted. They were used to embellish a painting, to create "jewels," or to fill in areas of color. Raised paste, which fired yellow in color, was applied in the form of dots, lines, and scrolls, and always covered with gold.

The silver in the bonbon bowl (left) and on the dresser set pieces (above) appear to be the same. However, the silver on the dresser set pieces must be periodically polished to retain their shine.

The border of this plate was created by covering the floral pattern and inner ring of dots and border band, as well as the center of the plate and handle, with a protective tar coating and dipping into hydrofluoric acid. The acid removed the glaze on the unprotected areas, producing a dull surface that contrasted with the glazed areas. Etched patterns always were covered with gold.

Silver and Platinum: Both metals fired to a shiny silver-color, but platinum did not tarnish.

Etching: Patterns where some of the glaze had been removed by dipping into hydrofluoric acid, leaving areas protected by tar (also called asphaltum) unaffected. Produced a design of contrasting shiny and dull surfaces that always was covered with gold.

Chasing: A design drawn with a fine agate point that produced a bright line on a matt-gold surface. Resembled engraving.

The bats on the rim of this candlestick were drawn with a fine agate point. Chased areas appeared bright against a matt gold surface.

The group of pansies on this plate is a decal. The background was enhanced with hand-painted color.

Mineral Transfers and Decals: Mass-produced printed pictures and outlines which could be enhanced with hand painting. Decal and mineral transfer pictures appear as a series of dots when viewed under a 10x magnifying glass. In contrast, painted areas are smooth or show visible brush strokes.

Outlined designs were meant to be filled with overglaze color. Some outlines were printed on carbons that were then traced by hand onto porcelain. These outlines usually have tell-tale signs by the unevenness of the line. Stamps were dipped into grounding oil first, stamped onto a porcelain surface, then dusted with powdered mineral paint and fired. The third type of outline design was decal.

It is often difficult, if not impossible, to determine with assurance whether a design has been stamped or is a pre-printed decal outline.

This stamp was one of many designs offered by china distributor W. A. Maurer. It matches the pattern on the cheese and cracker dish pictured on page 145. However, close visual inspection of the design on the porcelain provides no clue that its outline was stamped.

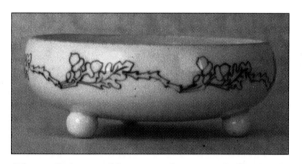

The outlining on this nut cup is uneven, indicating it was drawn by hand.

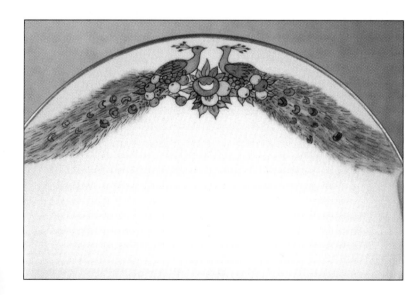

A decal of the peacock and fruit motif on this cake plate was fired in place, then filled in with overglaze color. Careful scrutiny with a magnifying loupe makes no revelation that the outline is a decal. Its discovery was accidental, pictured in **The China Painters' A-B-C** *by Mrs. C. C. Filkins (1915). Mrs. Filkins promoted the use of F. G. Coover's Black Outlines, and featured numerous examples of their offerings throughout her book.*

"To domesticate art and make it a part of
the household is one of the most strongly
pronounced tendencies of our time."

The Art Amateur, June 1879

Chapter One

The History of the American China Painting Movement

American painted porcelain was part of a vast consumer market during the Victorian era, and its prominence extended through the third decade of the twentieth century. Nearly ten million people visited the Philadelphia Centennial Exposition in 1876, where they were exposed to china painting for the first time at the Woman's Pavilion, and thousands eventually embraced it. Unlike other artforms, this was a medium with which people were intimately involved. China painting was done on common, functional objects beautified with subjects familiar to their everyday realm.

As an artform, painted porcelain successfully encompassed Aesthetic ideals first proposed by the Englishman William Morris (1834-1896). Morris, a poet, designer, craftsman, idealist, and social reformer, is credited with founding the Aesthetic Movement and calling attention to the need for art and beauty in all aspects of life. He proclaimed that everyday items should be nothing less than works of art. Hand-painted porcelains fulfilled his criteria of combining utility and artistry. Fifty years later, Evelyn Marie Stuart echoed Morris's philosophy in her article "America As A Ceramic Art Center," which was published in the May 1910 edition of *Fine Arts Journal*. Stuart wrote, ". . . perhaps after all no art is higher or truer than that which adds one virtue to another already established—beauty to utility." The decoration on porcelain was intended to provide the user more pleasure, thus elevating porcelain's status to a fine art.

While the extremely wealthy preferred hand-painted European porcelain, those in the middle and upper classes emulated the culture of the very rich with American painted pieces. These less expensive porcelains were either purchased from local studios, jewelry shops, or department stores, or painted by their own hands. In contrast, those in the lower classes used earthenwares and other inexpensive ceramics. If they had porcelain at all, it would have been items decorated with mass-produced decals, which were less costly.

Additionally, interior fashions created spaces customized for the integration of hand-painted porcelains. "Perhaps the architects of this country are in great measure responsible for this demand since in modern American homes there are innumerable little niches, pedestal and brackets that call for the use of decorative pieces of pottery or porcelain," suggested Stuart. From open transoms fitted with shelves to overmantels rising like balconied skyscrapers, each structure begged for objects to make rooms complete. Furniture reiterated interior architecture. Whatnots, sideboards, china cabinets, and vitrines did not look right unless filled to overflowing with layers of porcelain plates, jugs, vases, and covered boxes.

Floor plan and room description for
a two-story house from **Golden
Manual, or the Royal Road to
Success** by Henry Davenport
Northrop (1891).

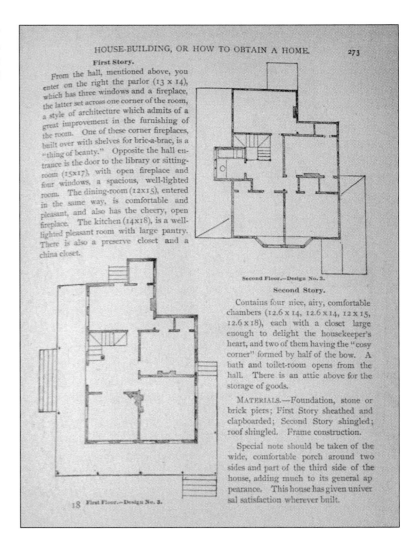

HOUSE-BUILDING, OR HOW TO OBTAIN A HOME.   273

First Story.

From the hall, mentioned above, you enter on the right the parlor (13 x 14), which has three windows and a fireplace, the latter set across one corner of the room, a style of architecture which admits of a great improvement in the furnishing of the room. One of these corner fireplaces, built over with shelves for bric-a-brac, is a "thing of beauty." Opposite the hall entrance is the door to the library or sitting-room (15x17), with open fireplace and four windows, a spacious, well-lighted room. The dining-room (12x15), entered in the same way, is comfortable and pleasant, and also has the cheery, open fireplace. The kitchen (14x18), is a well-lighted pleasant room with large pantry. There is also a preserve closet and a china closet.

Second Floor.—Design No. 3.

Second Story.

Contains four nice, airy, comfortable chambers (12.6 x 14, 12.6 x 14, 12 x 15, 12.6 x 18), each with a closet large enough to delight the housekeeper's heart, and two of them having the "cosy corner" formed by half of the bow. A bath and toilet-room opens from the hall. There is an attic above for the storage of goods.

MATERIALS.—Foundation, stone or brick piers; First Story sheathed and clapboarded; Second Story shingled; roof shingled. Frame construction.

Special note should be taken of the wide, comfortable porch around two sides and part of the third side of the house, adding much to its general appearance. This house has given universal satisfaction wherever built.

18   First Floor.—Design No. 3.

Frederick L. Grunewald, a Chicago-based china distributor and decorator, reported to the Ceramic Congress held in Chicago in 1893 that when china painting was first practiced in the United States, it was regarded as a passing fancy by many who were not directly involved in the field. In the paper that he read to the Congress he described the interrelation between culture, leisure, and financial independence for women, who, as a result of the Industrial Revolution and rising affluence for the middle class, no longer needed to work.

*"The introduction of this art into our homes gave us an idea
of leisure, culture and means. If china painting (I speak of it
only as an art practised by amateurs) had accomplished nothing more than to open to us the thought of studying the
products of the famous potteries of the world, it would have
been sufficient credit to it; but it has done more, we have
become convinced that there is other art besides that of oil
and water-colors—viz. that of ceramic colors applied to
unglazed and glazed pottery."*

By the turn of the twentieth century, over 25,000 people were painting dresser sets, tableware, and bibelots. "China painting by hand might almost be called an American art, so widely is it carried on and so readily appreciated in this country," wrote Stuart in "America As A Ceramic Art Center." Many porcelain artists remained amateurs in that they painted for pleasure rather than for profit, keeping their finished wares or distributing them to their relatives and close friends. Others marketed their creations through art studios, fine jewelry and department stores, art galleries, and art schools. Consequently, middle and upper class Americans adorned their homes with domestically decorated porcelain.

The changes occurring to china painting beginning in the second decade of the twentieth century, and its temporary decline, can be traced in the pages of *Keramic Studio*, a magazine devoted to china painting.★ Its co-founder and editor, Adelaide Alsop Robineau, herself a china painter-turned-art potter, wrote in the October 1914 editorial, ". . . nobody suspected that a monstrous, stupid war [World War I] would suddenly stop all economic life in Europe and disturb the business of neutral countries." At the time, most artists used art supplies and whiteware (undecorated, glazed white porcelain) imported from Germany, France, and Austria because the handful of porcelain manufacturers in the United States did not cater to this segment of the market. (American porcelain companies then, as now, concentrated their manufacturing on commercial products.) Robineau noted that the importation of French and German china had stopped entirely, admonishing that the supply on hand wouldn't last forever.

The war in Europe affected material imports, but it did not prevent fashion from crossing the Atlantic. At the time of William Morris's death in

"Suggestions for Transoms" from the February 1889 issue of **The Art Amateur.** *(Photo credit: The Newberry Library, Chicago)*

1896, the Arts and Crafts Movement was arising in America, as the Aesthetic Movement inspired by Morris was waning. Morris's talent for flat pattern design laid the groundwork for the conventional (i.e., geometric and abstract) style preferred by followers of the Arts and Crafts Movement, replacing naturalism in decorative arts. Art Deco design influences became entrenched in the mid-teens, creating a demand for simplified, streamlined, and stylized motifs.

★Keramic Studio *was published from May 1899 until May 1924, when the magazine was re-named* Design—Keramic Studio. *By 1930 articles on china decoration had ceased, although suppliers continued advertising.*

While Robineau was lamenting on the state of the art, the search for creative ideas continued. The Chicago-based china importer and art supply company, Thayer & Chandler, published *The China Painter Instruction Book* in 1914 to oblige this artistic quest. In their book, the company commented on the prevailing design trend. "The old-fashioned naturalistic style of china decoration is a thing of the past. . . . There can be no doubt that conventional work has come to stay . . ."

Nature remained the main inspirational source, but the interpretation of natural forms altered from imitation to invention. Natural forms were transformed into geometric patterns. "Nature furnishes the raw material, not the ready made design," wrote Henrietta Barclay Paist in *Design and the Decoration of Porcelain*, published by Keramic Studio Publishing Company two years later in 1916.

In her book, Paist reflected upon the American china painting movement. When painting on porcelain was introduced in this country, European immigrants who had trained in native factories gladly filled our need for technical instruction. They taught American artists to paint fruits and florals in a natural way. Paist and many others looked upon a naturalistic style as fraudulent, though many porcelain artists continued painting in this manner, old-fashioned as the style may have appeared.

Paist wrote that "we became 'degenerate copyists of copies.'" Porcelain transformed into art objects, rather than remained articles of service. "A piece of china was to us the same as canvas to the pictorial artist," she wrote; but "we have found ourselves, not as china painters, but as china decorators, to be a part of that great Industrial Army which is making itself felt in every department of the home all over the land . . . ." Little did Paist realize that this emphasis on industrial art and the commercial would eventually prove disastrous for china painters.

The simplicity of conventional designs was deceptive. Execution required painstaking perfection that was difficult to achieve. Such time-consuming processes naturally deserved equal compensation, but it became more difficult for porcelain artists to justify higher pricing. People did not want to pay more, despite the precision required to execute them. In 1917, one subscriber's lament was recorded in the editorial of the May issue of *Keramic Studio*.

"Just to give you an idea of the prices paid the worker: 10¢ a working for bread and butter plates, next size plates 12¢, next size 15¢ and so on. I know of this instance: a large French salad bowl, decorated in conventional basket motifs, all done in hard enamels with much gold, representing a good deal of work carefully done, sold for $4.50. Think of it, how can anyone make a living at such prices?"★

Although decals had been used since the mid-nineteenth century, the technique had not been employed on any great scale in America until the second decade of the twentieth century. Decals are copies of original artwork that are printed onto

★*The average weekly wage in 1917 was less than $16.*

paper or plastic sheets. Only one firing is required to fuse the picture with the glaze. Thus, the multiple production of a single design is easier, more consistent, and less expensive. The profit potential from mass marketing, and the standardization of quality that decals offered, began to outstrip the demand for hand painted porcelains. American companies began offering mass-produced, decal-decorated wares to service the expanding dinnerware market with a less expensive product. This kind of decoration can be recognized by its series of dots which can be seen when viewed under a magnifying glass or 10x loupe. Brush strokes may be apparent with hand painting. If the strokes were blended, the surface will appear smooth.

As women gained more freedom, along with broadened occupational opportunities and the right to vote, their interest in hand-painted china waned. During World War I, women spent their free time doing volunteer work to assist war efforts, rather than fulfilling artistic pursuits. After the war, the price of imports had increased to such an extent that it discouraged many from returning to the artform, or even taking it up in the first place. They preferred dancing and athletic activities to sedentary pursuits such as needlework, painting, and reading. They had less time to pursue hobbies that required as much time as did china painting, nor did their lives revolve around the home.

Many artists who had once embraced china painting wholeheartedly, could no longer compete financially. Fewer households could afford to employ, or even procure, the help necessary to allow them to pursue time-consuming interests and to stage the gastronomic feats and dinner parties as they had in Victorian times. Interiors also were simplifying. Gone were the layers of pattern and bric-a-brac. Hand-painted porcelain, once part of this splendid lifestyle, lost its allure and thus, its value. Porcelains were packed away, waiting for half a century or more to be rediscovered.

As the new millennium approaches, we now have the perspective to appreciate these forgotten treasures. No longer considered a craze or merely a pastime, American painted porcelain is gaining recognition as an artform and as an antique treasure. Readily available and reasonably priced, once again it is experiencing a resurgence.

TREATMENT OF DOOR AND VESTIBULE.

Drawing of a front hall from the
March 1888 issue of **The Art Amateur.**
(Photo credit: The Newberry Library, Chicago)

"IT SHOULD BE BORNE IN MIND OF ENTRANCES IN GENERAL
THAT, WHILE THE MAIN PURPOSE OF A DOOR IS TO ADMIT,
ITS SECONDARY PURPOSE IS TO EXCLUDE."

Edith Wharton and Ogden Codman, Jr.
"The Decoration of Houses," 1897

Chapter Two

Lasting Impressions: The Front Hall

Walking up to the entry of a typical Victorian home, one traversed several stairs and faced a fancy front door or pair of doors, inset with etched, leaded, or stained glass panels. A maid or butler would answer a ringing doorbell and screen callers, allowing entry into the front hall. The space, six to eight feet wide by twelve to twenty or more feet long, was a buffer zone dividing public from private. Those who were welcome guests were allowed to proceed to the parlor. Others, such as mail carriers, might never have attained the honor of venturing further.

Furnishing requirements were limited. All that was necessary was a place to sit while waiting, an umbrella stand, a hat rack known as a hall stand, a mirror, and a small table which held the card tray. Of all these items, the card tray assumed a pivotal role in facilitating the lady of the house to ascertain which visitors to receive.

The Custom of Calling

In the days before telephones, people kept in touch by making social calls. Calls could be a simple visitation of friends or a way of entering a new social circle. A call could be paid to issue an invitation, or as a reciprocating gesture after a dinner, for example. They also were made to convey congratulations, condolences, or get-well wishes, as the occasion required.

The calling ritual was governed by specific protocol. Visits were usually made in the afternoon, between the hours of noon and six. "Where one expects to touch upon reception hours, from three to five is usually a safe limit," wrote Maud C. Cooke in 1902 in *Our Deportment, or the Manners and Customs of Polite Society.* Those who lived in the country, where lifestyles tended to be less formal, could make calls any time in the afternoon, although "from two to five are the usual hours for paying visits," suggested Cooke. No calls were made before luncheon, unless they were less formal calls made by very close friends. These informal calls were not governed by the same social rules, however.

Isabella Beeton, author of *Mrs. Beeton's Book of Household Management,* which was first published in 1861, and underwent the subsequent printing of several editions, presented this practical advice.

> *"It is not advisable to take pet dogs into another lady's house, for there are people who have an absolute dislike to animals; besides this, there is always a chance of the animal breaking something, to the annoyance of the hostess. Except in the case of close friends or special invitation, little children should not accompany a lady in making morning calls."*

Initially, evening calls were rarely made by women. As more women worked or pursued outside activities, the acceptable hours for making calls shifted towards late afternoon and early evening. In the 1923, volume I edition of *Book of Etiquette* by Lillian Eichler, the author specifies that in the city, formal calls were made between 4:00 and 6:00 p.m. Men who worked during the day were allowed to make evening calls, between 8:00 and 9:30 p.m. In all cases, calls were to last no less than 15 minutes and no more than 45 minutes.

Women denoted one day a week when they were "at home." "The woman who professes a fondness for social intercourse nowadays sets aside a few hours of one afternoon in every week when she is prepared to see friends of both sexes and to offer them refreshment," wrote Helen L. Roberts in *Putnam's Handbook of Etiquette,* which was published in 1913. At-home cards were issued to friends and acquaintances who were expected to come; thus, the lady of the house could avoid unwanted guests.

Without telephones, people could not first ring and find out if the lady of the house was free. If calls were made on days other than what she specified, it was understood that a woman could be physically present but not "socially" at home. In other words, if she was involved in a project she could tell her maid or butler that she was not receiving visitors.

When friends and acquaintances made such calls, they left their cards for the hostess to review at her leisure. Those in the upper class had their names and addresses engraved on plain white or ivory stock. Their names were considered impressive enough. Many in the middle class preferred cards with colorful illustrations.

The card receiver was placed on a hall table, where visitors had a chance to discreetly peek at the names of other callers included in the social circle. Under no circumstances was the caller to present it directly to her hostess. A maid or butler carried the tray to the mistress of the house for her inspection.

Initially, a woman left one of her own cards and two of her husband's in the calling card tray: two for the lady of the house, the other for the lady's husband. Though her husband was rarely present, the woman who called was his representative. In this manner, social ties were maintained.

Card Trays

Card receivers became fashionable by the 1860s, and they remained a prominent feature in every middle and upper class entry hall for over half a century. As late as 1922, noted etiquette expert Emily Post wrote that the card tray was an essential item on every hall table. According to Post, when a doorbell rang, the servant presented the card tray to the visitor with his or her gloved left hand. She admonished that the servant never touch the card itself, for the card tray was to be carried to the lady of the house free of fingerprints.

Porcelain trays came in multiple sizes and shapes. Their decoration ranged from naturalistic florals to geometric conventional designs. Thus, card trays could be easily mistaken for other types of trays.

Today, such strict rules regarding visiting are not necessary. We expect people to telephone first instead of dropping in unexpectedly. Rather than butlers or maids, we have answering machines to "take calls" when we don't wish to be disturbed, and Caller ID to identify those whom we wish to ignore. Women use their cards to establish a business, rather than social, network.

Card tray; 7⅞"w x 6½"d; Wild roses executed in overglaze paints; burnished gold rim; Signed "M.E.M."; Blank: D & Co., France; ca. 1879–1900; $35–50.

Trays of similar dimension were listed also as manicure trays in china catalogs.

In fact, a majority of contemporary homes lack a front hall or separate reception area. Delivery personnel are content to leave packages outside one's front door, and those who deliver mail often do so without ever leaving their vehicles. Calling card trays, like the ritual of calling, have slipped quietly into a genteel past when people had time on their hands and less demands to fill it.

What characterizes a calling card tray? Size is the distinguishing factor. The card tray (center) is smaller than a comb and brush tray (left), but larger than a pin tray (right). On average they ranged from about 8 to 9 inches long by 5½ to 6½ inches wide. In comparison, sandwich trays could be 11½ inches long or longer, comb and brush trays 13 inches in length, and serving trays as much as 15½ inches long. Pin trays ranged from a mere 5 to 6 inches in length.

THE FURNISHING OF A SMALL APARTMENT.—THE PARLOR. (THE DINING-ROOM WAS SHOWN LAST MONTH.)

Drawing of a parlor from the November 1895 issue of **The Art Amateur.** *(Photo credit: The Newberry Library, Chicago)*

"THE REAL OBJECT OF A DRAWING-ROOM IS TO CHARM AT
THE FIRST LOOK, TO AMUSE AT THE SECOND."

The Art Amateur, September 1879

Chapter Three

Socializing with Society: The Parlor

After arriving to make a call and dropping the requisite number of three cards in the card tray, the maid or butler returned after presenting the card tray to the mistress of the house, and escorted guests to the parlor. For most middle class families, the parlor (which those in the upper classes called a drawing room) functioned as a combination family room and sitting room. "Here, 'beauty, sweetness, and light' are to culminate. The purpose of a drawing-room is relaxation and social enjoyment . . . in this room fancy reigns supreme . . . whatever of poetry, of art, or of culture there is in us will manifest itself in the fittings and accessories of the withdrawing-room," stated the anonymous author of "The Art of Furnishing: Part III. The Drawing-Room," which appeared in the September 1880 edition of *The Art Amateur*.

It was in this room that guests were received, light refreshments served, and small concerts and theatricals presented. Here, too, was where major family ceremonies occurred, including baptisms, engagement parties, weddings, and funeral viewings. Although male family members might use the room, it was considered within the woman's domain and decorated accordingly.

Painted porcelains could be found punctuating this room. Fireplaces might be surrounded with hand-painted tiles, inspired by designs featured in either *The Art Amateur*, a magazine devoted to the cultivation of household arts

Tiles; 6"w by 18"h; Hollyhocks executed in overglaze paints; Blank: none; ca. 1880–1900; $75-125.

Tiles; 6"w by 18"h; Irises executed in overglaze paints; Blank: none; ca. 1880–1900; $75-125.

which was published from 1879 to 1903, or *Keramic Studio*. Mantels, furniture with multiple shelves, such as whatnots and vitrines, and the tops of bookcases and tables were covered with decorative vases, plates, chocolate sets, bowls, and jardinieres. Porcelain was placed above window cornices and pelmets, and on open transoms above doorways.

Since the parlor was considered the most important room in the home, ostentation and abundance, which reflected a family's wealth and good taste, was accepted and expected. Grouping objects into patterned compositions where one piece did not predominate was an accomplishment in itself. "Apparent disorder is the highest art. Study well the disorder of your drawing-room," wrote the anonymous author of the column "Notes and Hints" in the September 1879 issue of *The Art Amateur*. Clarence Cook reiterated this thought in his book *The House Beautiful*, where he wrote that irregular arrangements averted monotony.

Hand-painted tiles drew attention to the fireplace, the focal point of domestic life. Thus, it was a room's central architectural feature. ". . . the tiles that border the opening . . . are the shining armor of the god of fire, and he likes to let his sparkling eye roam over them in the twilight . . .," wrote Clarence Cook in *The House Beautiful*.

"Design for Tile Fireplace Facing" from the April 1888 issue of **The Art Amateur.**
(Photo credit: The Newberry Library, Chicago)

Callers were seated in the parlor and were expected not to traverse the room or handle objects, as it was considered improper. Visual inspection revealed what the lady of the house wished her caller to know. In the case of porcelain, especially pieces painted by her own hand, they told of her talent and love of art, of her elevated lifestyle where utilitarian objects were transformed into artworks in their own right, and of her refinement. Additionally, they served as unique and personal counterpoints to mass-produced, machine-made and -decorated furnishings that dominated the room.

Whatnots: The Pride of the Parlor

The Victorian age was one of accumulation. An increase in wealth brought a corollary increase in leisure and discretionary income, which, in turn, created a demand for art and culture. From the upper classes to the middle classes, people wanted to surround themselves with furnishings that mirrored their wealth and artistic and cultural acquisitions. As a result furniture with shelves, tiers, and niches was designed to accommodate this accumulation.

As architecture became elaborate, so did interiors. Rooms were meant to entertain, instruct, and elevate through their layers of pattern, texture, and bric-a-brac.

Nowhere was the commitment to ornament more prevalent than in the parlor.

During the first half of the nineteenth century the parlor was the focal point of family life. But by the latter half of the century, its purpose was less functional and more decorative—a repository of treasured possessions. The parlor became a family museum of prized items, memorabilia, and collectibles, curated by the mistress of the house.

"Even here the ornaments for the sake of ornament alone should find no place. The vases should be of a character to hold flowers, the candlesticks to give light…"

"CONCERNING THE DRAWING ROOM," BY OLIVER COLEMAN
The House Beautiful MAGAZINE, NOVEMBER 1897

The whatnot was one piece of furniture created expressly for the purpose of displaying precious objects. The whatnot was a triangular-shaped, open set of shelves usually made of mahogany, black walnut, or rosewood, and embellished with fretwork. The shelves graduated in size, beginning with the smallest at the top. Meant to fit into a corner, it could be either freestanding or wall-hung. Whatnots and their elegant counterparts, *étagères*, first appeared during the Rococo revival period of the 1850s and 1860s, in a style characterized by an abundance of ornate carving and curves.

An *étagère* was a larger version of the humbler whatnot of the middle classes and rural households. Additionally, it varied from the whatnot in that it was meant to be placed flat against a wall. Next to the center table, the whatnot or *étagère* held the greatest importance in the parlor, and both were essentially status symbols. Either one of these shelved pieces of furniture could be incorporated into an "art corner," filled with books, natural specimens, busts of famous writers, copies of well-known sculptures, or china.

The objects on display were meant to entice closer visual examination by guests, although

Vase forms came from China, where they were esteemed for their purely aesthetic qualities. Porcelain vases remained a decorative extravagance when they were initially introduced in Europe. To the Victorian mindframe, particularly one that respected the combination of beauty with utility, vases were adapted to hold cut flowers and plants by the mid-nineteenth century.

they were not allowed to touch anything. These pieces were placed to stimulate conversation and convey subtle messages about the family's taste, education, and adventures. For example, a hand-painted porcelain vase would have told visitors that the lady of the house was a cultured individual and a competent artist.

Vase; 6⅛"h; Violets and ground colors executed in overglaze paints; burnished gold handles and rim; Signed: "E. Sprecht"; Blank: none; ca. 1880s; $35-55.

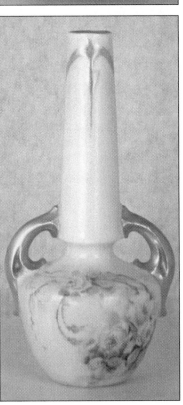

Vase; 7"h; Roses and ground colors executed in overglaze paints; burnished gold rim, accents, handles; Blank: none; ca. 1900-1920; $35-55.

Vase; 7⅛"h; Roses and ground colors executed in overglaze paints; burnished gold rim; Blank: Belleek palette, Lenox; 1906-1924; $250-300.

Vase, 5"h; Forget-me-nots and ground color executed in overglaze paints; burnished gold rim and handle; Blank: Royal wreath, O. & E. G.; 1898-1918; $35-55.

Vase; 8½"h; Roses and ground colors executed in overglaze paints; burnished gold rim; Signed: "J. P." Blank: Fraunfelter China, Ohio; 1925; $35-55.

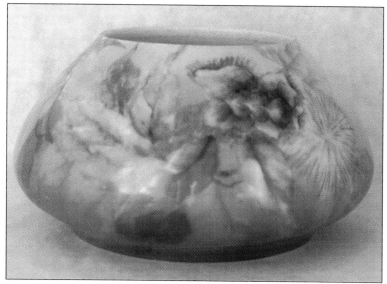

Vase; 6½"dia by 3½"h; Chinquapins and ground colors executed in overglaze paints; Blank: none; ca. 1900-1925; $35-45.

Dragon-handled ewer; 9¾"h; Mountain primrose and dragon body executed in overglaze paints; ground color executed in matt paint; burnished gold handle, neck, and base; Signed: "K. B. R."; Blank: none; ca. 1880-1890; $100-125.

"All china painters will remember the shapes with dragon handles that were used during the reign of the Royal Worcester imitations. They are now to be found on the top shelves of most china shops . . ." **Keramic Studio, May 1899**

Incense jar; 4½"dia by 3⅛"h; Conventional-style clover border design executed in burnished gold; ground color executed in overglaze paint; burnished gold top; (Also listed as a rose jar in china catalogs. This jar was probably used for incense because of interior residue.) Signed: "Xmas 1926, From Emma"; Blank: Prov. Sxe. E. S. Germany; $35-55.

Foot Fetish

One ornamental fad of the nineteenth and even the twentieth centuries was the display of small china forms shaped like women's shoes. Such seemingly banal objects carried with it coquettish connotations. When women wore long skirts that covered their legs, the quick glimpse of a woman's boot as she stepped into her carriage, or the exposure of her ankle during a skating party, was arousing to a man. Yet foot fetishes, particularly the love of shoes, dates back even farther. The Dutch

Shoe; 3⅞"w by 2⅛"h; Forget-me-nots executed in overglaze paints; burnished gold rim and heel; Stamped: "Osborne"; Blank: none; ca. 1910-1930; $35-55.

Shoe; 3¾"w by 2⅛"h; Pansies executed in overglaze paints: burnished gold rim and heel; Stamped: "Pasco"; Blank: none; ca. 1910-1930; $35-55.

Although these shoes are not identified with a manufacturer's mark that might verify a date, based on their style and decoration an approximate time period can be assigned. Their more rectangular form and chunkier heel are reflective of styles popular from around 1910 to as late as the 1930s.

Flowers contained their own intrinsic symbolism, conveying the objects they decorated with unique meanings and silent messages. Forget-me-nots and pansies represented remembrance. Both types of flowers were used as decorative motifs on a variety of items, from greeting cards to calling cards. Perhaps these shoes were initially given as gifts.

and English made ceramic shoes of delftware in the 1600s. In Germany ceramic shoes were presented to newlyweds as fertility charms. While many women have loved shoes and amassed pairs the way others amass collections, at the extreme were women such as Imelda Marcos and Eva Perón whose hundreds of pairs required specially constructed closets. Porcelain shoes are simply easier to exhibit, and were usually purchased as a single shoe, seldom as a pair.

Overdone Overmantels

Another Victorian invention that resulted from their passion for accumulating possessions, and their desire to show them off, was the elaborate overmantel. Though not as important as it had been in the nineteenth century, the mantel remained a focal point, around which the family congregated. "The mantel-piece ought to second the intention of the fire-place as the center of the family life . . .

Vase; 15"h; Autumn landscapes, wild roses, and ground colors executed in overglaze paints; burnished gold rim and handles; Signed: "Thonander, Chicago" (John Thonander, 1910-1912); Blank: crown, fish, laurel, Austria; $475-575.

Large vases, sometimes filled with plants, dried grasses, or peacock feathers, were placed on hearths in front of fireplaces.

Vase; 10¾"h; Wild carrots and ground colors executed in overglaze paints; burnished gold rim; Signed: "M J Leber, 1915"; Blank: Crown, H & Co., Selb, Bavaria; $150-175.

Tall vases were placed on mantels to emphasize its height, as well as to create a focal point.

There ought, then, to be gathered on the shelf, or shelves, over the fire-place, a few beautiful and chosen things," wrote Clarence Cook in *The House Beautiful*.

Towering shelving arrangements rose vertically above the mantel shelf solely for the exhibition of ornamental objects, such as candlesticks, plates, and vases, "the main point being that they should be things to lift us up . . . things we are willing to live with, and to have our children grow up with, and that we never can become tired of," wrote Cook. A century later, these same carefully chosen items still charm and captivate, and for those fortunate to have grown up with pretty porcelains, have carried this tradition to their offspring.

Green Dreams

During the nineteenth century, many people focused their attention on the natural world. As mechanization and industrialization increasingly encroached on people's lives, in an attempt to achieve a balance with nature, they filled their homes with foliage. Fields of flowers and greenery bloomed on carpets, and floral wallpapers surrounded occupants with sylvan bowers.

Greenery and live plants connected a family with the outdoor environment and paid deference to their love of nature. They also acted as room fresheners and decorative accents. Ivy was trained to climb interior walls, encircling windows and doors. Plants were dotted throughout rooms, on furniture specifically designed for their display, or on the floor. Some plant stands held a number of containers. Other furniture, such as the fern table, gave special status to individual plants.

Jardiniere; 5½"h; Geraniums and ground colors executed in overglaze paints; Blank: crown, crossed scepters, Rosenthal, Bavaria; ca. 1901-1933; $50-75.

Jardiniere; 8⅜"dia; Floral forms executed in colored enamels; border designs executed in overglaze paints; Signed: "Clara M. Smith"; Blank: Belleek palette, Lenox; ca. 1920-1930; $65-95.

Various containers were available to house plants and bouquets, including cache-pots, jardinieres, planters, ferneries, and vases. In Europe and England, terra cotta planters were meant to be placed inside cache-pots. (The name cache-pot means "pot-hider.") Jardinieres were decorative planters that either had a hole in the bottom, or came with a pierced liner to provide drainage. The American term for both types of containers was planter, although old china catalogs used the term "jardiniere."

Jardiniere; 10¾"h; Conventional-style birds, flowers, and butterflies executed in overglaze paints; burnished gold ground and feet; Signed: "Clara M. Smith, April 14, 1925"; Blank: crown, H & Co., Selb, Bavaria; $275–375.

Jardiniere; 5½"h; Floral forms executed in colored enamels; burnished gold rim, border, and feet; Signed: "Clara M. Smith, January 1928"; Blank: Belleek palette, Lenox; $65–115.

Ferneries or fern pots were meant only for the display of ferns. These types of containers could be low bowls or hanging vases. Vases usually were more slender than jardinieres and planters. They could be used by themselves as decorative accents, or filled with cut flowers.

At Your Service

Just before guests arrived for an afternoon call, the parlor's shades were drawn. Candles, lamps, and fireplaces were lit, or electric lights turned on, to create the proper atmosphere.

The hostess's duties included greeting each guest, making introductions, and drawing new arrivals into conversation with the others so that she could be free to greet the next guest. Political, religious, and controversial subjects were taboo, as were references to the deceased when making condolence calls. Visitors ". . . should not, unless gifted with rare tact, make any reference to the death but should rather speak of cheerful things," wrote Lillian Eichler in volume one of *Book of Etiquette.*

Calls lasted from no less than fifteen minutes to no more than

"Do not take children while making formal visits. They are often an annoyance, and always a check upon conversation. If they must be taken, do not allow them to meddle with anything in the room, nor to interrupt the conversation. Neither should they be permitted to handle the belongings, or finger the attire, of callers at the house."

MAUD C. COOKE, *Our Deportment, or Manners and Customs of Polite Society,* 1902

three-quarters of an hour. During that time the hostess served a choice of drinks and food from a variety of tableware, all of which could have been hand-painted porcelain. The hostess would establish herself at the tea table, where she would offer refreshments to her guests. "Tea tables are unusually pretty these days, and no place is quite so satisfactory to show off one's latest table accessories and dainty gowns, no place do my lady's dainty jewelled hands appear to greater advantage, than when presiding at her informal five o'clock tea," wrote Ellye Howell Glover in "*Dame Curtsey's*" *Book of Party Pastimes for the Up-to-Date Hostess* (1912). Ordinarily, hot breads, small sandwiches, and cake would be offered to accompany tea. In Glover's book, she presented a menu of toasted crackers with butter or cheese, the "thinnest of sandwiches," candied orange and lemon peel, and ginger and oyster crackers dipped in melted chocolate. Other authors mention bouillon and salads as well.

More elaborate receptions, which then were set up in the dining room, included a choice of coffee, hot chocolate, lemonade, or punch, in addition to tea, hot and cold breads, bonbons, ices, and a fruit salad. However, guests were counted upon to limit their selections and portions. "It is not expected that guests will indulge themselves in a liberal meal at an afternoon reception. The partaking of an ice, of a cup of tea and a cake, or of a cup of coffee and a sandwich is a sufficient response to the hospitality offered," wrote Emily Holt in volume two of *Encyclopaedia of Etiquette*.

Sidney Morse, author of *Household Discoveries*, took a more practical viewpoint. He wrote, "Have, if possible, in one corner of the room a small, low table with an alcohol lamp and suitable tea things for making a cup of tea without going for it to the kitchen. This simple expression of hospitality gives a note of good cheer that is much needed in modern social life. There need be no formality suggested by a cup of tea offered to a caller even in the most quiet neighborhoods, and having all of the needful articles at hand helps to give the serving of tea an air of grace and naturalness."

Afternoon Receptions

Long before the days of telephones and television, visiting a friend was an occasion for sharing conversation and one's prized possessions, such as porcelain. The decoration of the parlor, and the serving of refreshments, afforded hostesses with the perfect environment and opportunity to display and use her hand-painted treasures.

Biscuit jar; 6⅛"dia by 5"h; Burnished gold palm tree design and handles, overglaze paint outline; Blank: crown, crossed sceptors, Rosenthal, Selb-Bavaria; ca. 1908-1920; $50-75.

Biscuit jar; 7⅛"dia by 5½"h; Burnished gold rim, handles, base, and "CMS" monogram (porcelain artist Clara M. Smith); Blank: Royal wreath, O. & E. G., Austria; 1898-1918; $50-75.

Double-handled sandwich tray; 19¼"w by 6¼"d; Burnished gold rim, handles, and "CMS" monogram (porcelain artist Clara M. Smith); Blank: crowned double-headed bird, MZ, Austria; ca. 1884-1909; $55-75.

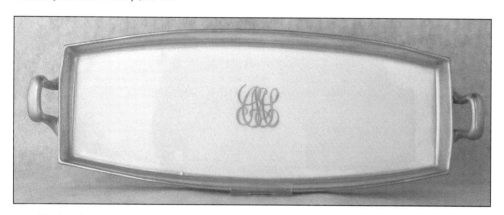

Double-handled sandwich tray; 11⅝"w by 4"d; Burnished gold rim, handles, and "CMS" monogram (porcelain artist Clara M. Smith); Blank: none; ca. 1920-1930; $45-55.

Double-handled cake plate; 11⅛"dia; Waterlilies and ground colors executed in overglaze paints; burnished gold rim and handles; Signed: "E.W."; Blank: none; ca. 1900-1920; $45-65.

Double-handled cake plate; 9½"d; Platinum wild carrot design, scrolls, rim, and handles; Signed: E.C.B.";
Blank: Germany; ca. 1891-1914; $45-55.

Matches bonbon bowl pictured on page 44.

Double-handled cake plate; 9⅛"dia; Stylized bird on a flowering cherry tree branch executed in overglaze paints; burnished gold rim and scrolls; Signed: "CD 1878"; Blank: none; $45-65.

This is a very early piece of American painted porcelain, decorated only two years after the china painting movement was launched in this country.

Double-handled individual cake plate or cookie tray; 6¾"dia; Conventional-style florals and basket executed in overglaze paints; burnished gold rim and handles; Signed: "Edith Kredell"; Blank: UNO-IT, Favorite Bavaria; ca. 1910-1920; $20-30.

Double-handled individual cake plate or cookie tray; 7⅛"dia; Border design of roses executed in overglaze paints; burnished gold rim, handles, and band; Blank: Limoges, France; ca. 1891-1918; $20-30.

Double-handled individual cake plate or cookie tray; 6⅝"dia; Poppies and ground colors executed in overglaze paints; burnished gold rim and handles; Stamped: "Kayser's Studio, Milwaukee, Wis." (Mrs. Magdalena Kayser, ca. 1910-1915); Blank: Favorite, Bavaria; $15-22.

Covered bonbon box; 8"dia by 4½"h; Yellow roses and ground colors executed in overglaze paints; burnished gold rims and bands; Signed: "R. STMD"; Blank: ADK, Limoges, France; ca. 1890s–1910; $150–225.

Covered bonbon box; 4¾"dia by 4¼"h; Art Nouveau-style design outlined in overglaze paint and embellished with burnished gold; ground covered with overglaze paint; Signed: "FWFW 1910(?)"; Blank: ADK, France; ca. 1890s–1910; $50–60.

Bonbon bowl; 7¾"dia; Conventional butterfly design executed in overglaze paints, mother-of-pearl luster, and burnished gold; panels of matt blue paint; mother-of-pearl luster interior; burnished gold borders; Signed: "E. W. Misner"; Blank: Favorite, Bavaria; ca. 1908–1920; $65–85.

Double-handled bonbon bowl; 6"dia; Conventional-style lilies, acanthus design, and ground color executed in overglaze paints; mother-of-pearl luster interior; burnished gold ground, scrolls, and handles; Signed: "Bard, 1909" (Isadore Bardos); Stamped: "Stouffer" (Stouffer Studio, Chicago); $55–75.

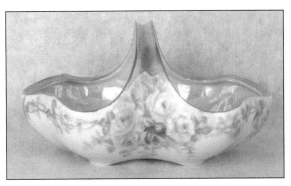

Bonbon basket; 7"w by 5"d by 3¾"h; Roses and ground colors executed in overglaze paints; mother-of-pearl luster interior; burnished gold rim and handles; Signed: "B. E. Tulmage"; Blank: wreath and star, R. S. Germany; ca. 1904-1938; $55-75.

Double-handled bonbon bowl; 6"dia; Platinum wild carrots, scrolls, rim, and handles; Signed: "E.C.B."; Blank: Germany; ca. 1891-1914; $15-25. Matches cake plate pictured on page 41.

Cooky basket; 7½"w by 5¼"d by 2½"h; Daisies and ground color executed in overglaze paints, burnished gold rim, border and handle; (Listed as a spoon basket in earlier china catalogs); Signed: "ALICE KISS, NOV 1920" Blank: Noritake, Nippon; $45-60.

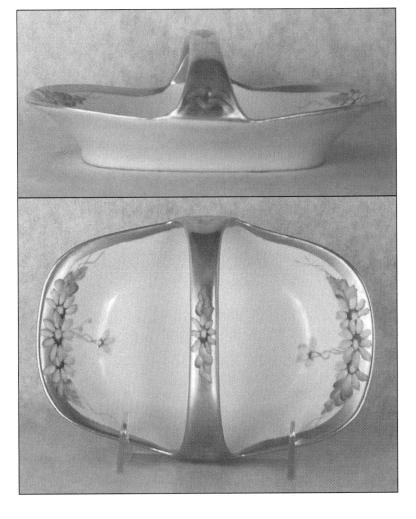

Tea sandwiches would be served from double-handled oblong sandwich trays, packaged in sets with six individual, 6-inch diameter plates called "bread-and-butter plates," or from sandwich baskets. Biscuit jars held sweet crackers or cookies, the word "biscuit" having a British origin.

Cake plates had pierced double handles and averaged between 9¼ inches to 10¼ inches in diameter. Individual cookie trays (sometimes spelled "cooky") were smaller versions of cake plates, ranging from 6½ inches to 7¼ inches in diameter. Accompanying bonbons were placed in shallow bowls, covered boxes, or baskets.

"Orchids are just now the popular flowers for dessert and ice-cream plates ..."

The Art Amateur
NOVEMBER 1888

Double-handled cake plate, 9½"dia; Orchids and ground colors executed in overglaze paints; burnished gold rim and handles; Blank: crown, Queen Louise, J & C, Bavaria; ca. 1902; $45-55.

Orchids were a favored motif for dessert porcelains because of their association with vanilla flavoring. Of the 35,000 species of orchids, only vanilla orchids produce edible fruit. These are found in rain forests of the Caribbean, Central America, the southeastern coast of Mexico, and the northernmost latitudes of South America.

The Totonacs, whose descendents still live in the Mexican state of Veracruz, were the first to process vanilla beans by fermentation at least a millennium ago. Their discovery is remarkable since neither the flower nor fruit of the vanilla orchid exude the distinct vanilla scent or flavor. The Totonacs used vanilla as a flavoring, perfume, medicine, insect repellent, and aphrodisiac.

Although vanilla was brought to Europe by Spanish colonists in 1510, vanilla reached the United States in a roundabout way. Thomas Jefferson discovered this flavoring while serving as ambassador to France, and had some imported here when he returned after 1789. In the early part of the nineteenth century, at a presidential dinner, Dolley Madison served vanilla ice cream, creating a vogue that lasted for a century. Thus, the connection between orchids and desserts flavored with vanilla was established.

Tea Time

Dutch ships gave Europe its initial taste of tea when it brought the first shipment from China around 1610, and it was the Dutch who established tea-drinking in New Amsterdam (later, New York City). The British continued the tradition when they settled here.

Tea remained a status symbol because of its high price. In the eighteenth century, porcelain, another expensive and coveted commodity, was used with increasing frequency to serve tea because its white color enhanced the color of the brew, and also for its insulating properties.

The first teacups actually were small bowls without handles. They date back to the middle of the ninth century when the Chinese first employed (and still do) porcelain containers. Although foreign to contemporary drinkers, the rationale for drinking tea in cups without handles was simple: If the cup was too hot to hold, then the tea was too hot to drink. Teapot forms often were based on silver models and followed prevailing stylistic trends. Other porcelain tea accouterments included sugar "dishes"—which were shallow dishes and circular bowls with or without lids, cream jugs, a slop basin for the dregs, and tea canisters.

North Americans emulated British style. The teapot held the center of attention, and teacups and saucers were arranged in orderly, circular rows around the teapot. First the teapot was warmed with scalding water. Loose tea leaves were placed in the teapot or in an infuser, and boiling water poured on top. The tea was allowed to steep from five to seven minutes. The tea was poured over a tea strainer resting on top of another hot teapot to filter any loose tea leaves.

Afternoon tea, served on a portable tea table, brought elegance into a woman's day. Precious heirlooms were taken out and used. In the 1880s and 1890s, these heirlooms might be decorated by the hostess's own hands, or by one of her accomplished friends. The following suggestion was written by M. B. Alling in the January 1890 edition of *The Art Amateur*:

"Now and then invite your friends for an evening, or to an afternoon tea, that they may see what you have been doing, and I am sure you will not complain of a lack of encouragement from them. The admiration called forth by your dainty cups, in which the fragrant beverage is served, and the charming bread-and-butter plates—all specimens of your handiwork, will warm your heart with honest pleasure. Now that the tea-table has become a necessity in every lady's drawing-room there is an opportunity given not only for the display of individual talent and taste, but for their application to practical use."

Four-piece tea set; tray, 11¼"dia; teapot (holds 24 oz.); covered sugar; creamer; Roses and ground colors executed in overglaze paints; burnished gold rims and borders, handles, and spout; Signed: "C. E. Tolehard, 1914"; Blank: crowned double-headed bird, MZ, Austria; $225-275.

Tabletop; 11⅜"dia; Daisies and ground colors executed in overglaze paints; burnished gold rim; Signed: "E. Miler"; Blank: T & V rectangle, Limoges, France; ca. 1892–1907; $75–100.

Tabletop; 9¼"dia; Seashells and ground colors executed in overglaze paints with white enamel highlights; burnished gold rim; Signed: "EdiTH SmiTH"; Blank: none; ca. 1900–1925; $65–85.

Dessert plate and tea strainer; plate, 7"dia; tea strainer, 6¼"w; Roses and ground color executed in overglaze paints; burnished gold rims, scrolled detailing, and monogram; Signed: "L. V. C."; Blank: plate: T & V rectangle, Limoges, France, Depose; tea strainer, none; ca. 1892–1907; plate, $15–25; tea strainer, $25–35.

Cup and saucer; Roses and wild roses executed in overglaze paints; burnished gold border ground and handle; Signed: "M. N. Stenger"; Blank: Germany; ca. 1891–1914; $25–35.

Cup and saucer; Nasturtiums and ground colors executed in overglaze paints; burnished gold rims and handle; Blank: Haviland, Limoges, France; ca. 1894–1931; $25–35.

Cup and saucer; Lilacs and ground colors executed in overglaze paints; burnished gold rims and handle; Blank: Haviland, France; ca. 1894–1916; $25–35.

Cup and saucer; Waterlilies and ground colors executed in overglaze paints; burnished gold rims and handle; Blank: Haviland, France; ca. 1894–1916; $25–35.

Cup and saucer; Roses and ground colors executed in overglaze paints; burnished gold rims and handle; mother-of-pearl luster interior; Blank: Favorite, Bavaria; ca. 1908–1918; $25–35.

Cup and saucer; Conventional-style fruit, color band, and ground color executed in overglaze paints; burnished gold borders, rims, and handle; Blank: UNO-IT, Favorite, Bavaria; ca. 1908-1920; $25-35.

Teapot stand; 6¾"dia; Conventional-style cherry design executed in overglaze paints; burnished gold rim; Signed: "M. H. WENTE, 1916"; Blank: crown and shield, Bavaria; $35-45.

Teapot stand; 6¼"dia; Conventional-style poppies and ground colors executed in overglaze paints; burnished gold rim; Signed: "N. O. BENDER"; Blank: none; ca. 1905-1920; $35-45.

Teapot stand; 6⅞"dia; Stork on a flowering branch and ground color executed in overglaze paints; burnished gold rim; Signed: "Charlotte Stephens (?) 4. 25"; Blank: Japan; $35–45.

Porcelain tea sets included a teapot, creamer, sugar bowl, cups and saucers, and a serving tray. A hostess might substitute a teapot stand for a serving tray, and she might want to include a porcelain tea strainer. There were even porcelain tea bells to ring for tea, which then would be brought in by a servant.

"A welcome addition to the tea-table … is a tea strainer with a drip bowl, the two forming one article. There is room for small flowers, or it may be simply tinted and gilded, and have a monogram in gold and enamel."

The Art Amateur
DECEMBER 1896

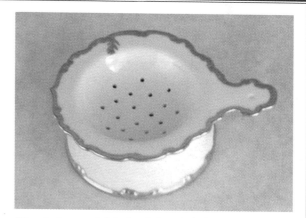

Tea strainer and drip bowl; Burnished gold rims; Signed: "Anne W. Breinin"; Blank: none; ca. 1900–1950; $35–45.

Five O'Clock Tea

Dialogues for Young People's Societies, circa 1911

Mrs. Long, young housewife. Mrs. Klock, Mrs. Knight, and Mrs. Todd, friends of Mrs. Long. Ladies are dressed for tea. Scene is parlor of Mrs. Long. Table neatly spread, four chairs. Picture on the wall with "Home sweet Home" on it.

Mrs. Long (*arranging dishes on table*). My first Five O'clock Tea! I wonder how it will be and what they will say of my furniture, tables and china. (*Looking around room.*) Everything looks neat and tidy. That "Home sweet Home" is inviting and spreads coziness and geniality about me. I always have loved a cozy little room with nice furniture and tasty arrangement, and I am sure they must like it too. Now let me see, did I forget anything? There are the cups and saucers, the spoons, the sugar, the cookies and cake. Yes, everything is on the table except the tea; but that I'll make when they are here. The tea kettle is simmering on the stove. (*Looking through window, sighing.*) And now I wish they would come. It seems so reckless of them to let me wait so long, and I am getting a little nervous. (*Door bell rings.*) Hello! there is one of them at least. (*Opens door.*) How do you do, Mrs. Klock. (*Enter Mrs. Klock, bowing.*)

Mrs. Klock: How do you do, Mrs. Long.

Mrs. Long: Thank you, quite well, how are you?

Mrs. Klock: Same. Thank you. And how is everything? My! Don't this look lovely!

Mrs. Long: Glad you like it. Please have a chair. (*Mrs. Klock sits.*) How is everything at home?

Mrs. Klock: Oh, they are all right. My husband is at his office as usual, and the children are at school—that is they were when I left. At this time they probably are at home. Oh my, how tired I am!

Mrs. Long: Why? Have you been shopping this afternoon?

Mrs. Klock: Indeed! Just imagine where I have been. I was at (*name four or five local merchants.*) looking for a rug. And then I went to (*name local baker.*) inquiring for the price of creamery butter. Just think of it, they ask 33 cents a pound! Isn't that a horrible price? On what do these people expect us to live if they keep on raising their prices that way? On wind? My husband says its all on account of the trust, they have trusts in everything and don't trust anybody. Now isn't that queer?

Mrs. Long: I should think so. So you were looking at rugs. Do you want to buy a new one for your parlor?

Mrs. Klock: For my sitting room! That rug in the parlor is allright and will do for a time yet. I bought it at (*name local dealer*) for $55 at a bargain. They say there is some smyrna in it, and considering the price I paid, it ought to be.

Mrs. Long: It is without doubt a beautiful rug. (*Looking down at her rug.*) What do you think this one here costs?

Mrs. Klock: (*Looking down.*) That one? Oh dear, you have got one, too. How queer of me not seeing it when I came in. (*Bending down and feeling at rug with fingertips.*) Where did you buy it?

Mrs. Long: At (*name local dealer.*) They say it is very stylish and my husband likes it so much.

Mrs. Klock: Oh, well, that doesn't amount to much what they tell you. They want to sell their goods and consequently are obliged to praise all their trash or people wouldn't buy it.

Mrs. Long: (*with embarrassed feeling.*) Trash! Do you call this trash?

Mrs. Klock: O dear, no! It is such a beautiful rug as one can get for the money, I am sure. And how nice patterns it has got! Almost like the one Mrs. Geering has got, and she only paid $24 for her's.

Mrs. Long: Well, this one costs $64.

Mrs. Klock: (*looking down.*) Is that possible? Why, then it costs more than mine. How can that be? Oh dear! How tired I am. I wish I had some tea.

Mrs. Long: (*rising*) I'll get you some. Please excuse me for a moment. (*Exit.*)

Mrs. Klock: How silly that woman is! Invites me to tea and doesn't give me any without reminding her first. Oh, I am nearly starved. (*Looking down, laughing.*) And the idea of telling me that she paid $64 for this rag carpet. Why, I can buy one like this at (name local dealer) for $18.43, but it would look to (sic) shabby for my sitting room. Why must she lie to me? It's an insult to tell me that, for I know better. Why must such people always bragg (sic) about their rags? (*Enter Mrs. Long with teapot in hand.*) Oh, what a lovely teapot you have! I am sure that looks like china.

Mrs. Long: (*amusedly.*) Maybe it is. (*Pouring in tea, two cups.*)

Mrs. Klock: How good of you! I am sure I will like your tea. We always buy our tea of (*local dealer*) for a dollar a pound. We use the monsoon black, for I hate the taste of green tea. I don't see how people can drink it.

Mrs. Long: (*in terror.*) Oh, you must excuse me, this tea is not good. (*Pouring tea back into pot.*) I'll go and make some better.

Mrs. Klock: Why, what is the matter? Give it here, I'll taste it.

Mrs. Long: No, never mind, I know it is not good—not black enough. I'll have some new tea ready in a moment. (*Exit.*)

Mrs. Klock: Shouldn't wonder if she had green tea in that pot. That would be just like her, brewing broth instead of wholesome tea. Now, here I sit still starving for refreshment and can't get a cup of tea. People who haven't got any senses should not invite others to tea. And I bet she is using tea leaves which you can buy at (*local dealer*) for 25 cents a pound. It would be just like her. (*Door bell.*) There! Somebody is coming. Wonder who it is.

Mrs. Long: (*showing in Mrs. Night.*) Just walk in Mrs. Night, you will find Mrs. Klock in the parlor. How glad I am that you have come to see me at my first tea.

Mrs. Night: (*to Mrs. Klock.*) How do you do? Glad to meet you. Isn't this fine weather we are having?

Mrs. Klock: I should say so. But how it makes a person feel tired.

Mrs. Long: Now, you ladies must excuse me, for I am going to bring in the tea.

Mrs. Night: Certainly, my dear, certainly. Don't be in a hurry with your tea, I have genial company in Mrs. Klock. (*Exit Mrs. Long.*) You are tired, you say? How does that come?

Mrs. Klock: I was shopping this afternoon and dropped in here for a cup of tea, but do I get any? She brought the pot in just before you came and when I intimated that I abhor green tea, she poured it back again and went out. Now I am starving for tea and don't get any. If there is one thing I hate in a woman, it's dawdling and sluggishness. And just imagine! She told me that she paid $64 for this rag under your feet!

Mrs. Night: The idea! For that thing? Why, Mrs. Todd has got one just like it and she bragged to me about buying it for $17.35 at (*name local dealer.*) Well, what does she know about rugs! They are both young and believe every word dealers will tell them in order to get rid of their rummage. (*Walking up to table.*) Is that china? (*Takes cup in hand and examines it.*)

Mrs. Klock: China! I bet they haven't got a piece of china in the house. I can see it from

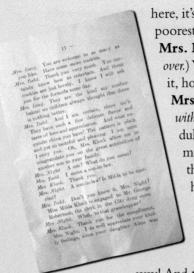

here, it's semi-porcelain of the poorest kind.

Mrs. Night: (*Handing cup over.*) You are right. Just lift it, how heavy it is.

Mrs. Klock: (*Sounding cup with tip of finger.*) And how dull it sounds! There is no more china in that cup than there is on my head. Here, put it back again. (*Mrs. Night puts cup back on table and sits.*) Why must people bragg (sic) that way! And then the furniture—do you notice anything valuable in this room?

Mrs. Night: Not a thing. Everything is of the cheapest kind, probably gotten from a second-hand-store, and varnished up to look like new. Well, I say it takes her quite long to brew that tea.

Mrs. Klock: Maybe she hasn't got black tea in the house and has to run to the store first in order to get it. Shouldn't wonder.

Mrs. Night: Most likely. Now if I am particular in one thing it is tea; it has to be of the right kind and of the proper strength or I will not touch it. She has been teaching school all her girl days, what can you expect of her.

Mrs. Klock: (*Walking up to table and looking at cookies, coming back.*) I thought so. She got them from the bakery.

Mrs. Night: (*Walking up to table and tasting cookies.*) Sure enough! And molasses cookies at that, made of flour and dark New Orleans molasses. If there is anything I abhor it is molasses cookies. (*Door bell. Mrs. Night slips back to Chair.*) There!

Mrs. Klock: And no tea ready to serve!

(*Mrs. Long appears with teapot in hand, showing Mrs. Todd in.*)

Mrs. Long: Have a chair and make yourself at home, Mrs. Todd. The other ladies will be delighted with your amiable company while I serve tea. (*Serves tea and cookies while others talk.*)

Mrs. Todd: How do you do, ladies? Quite comfortable, I see. How exquisite everything is in here. Dear Mrs. Long, your parlor is a paradise.

I always like to call on young housewives, they are so effectionate, so tender, so refined and know how to make things pleasant for their guests. Don't you, ladies?

Mrs. Klock, Mrs. Night: Certainly, Certainly.

Mrs. Todd: And all things look so new and have such a freshness about them. There's nothing lovelier than a young housewife inmidst of her new household. It's the picture of comfort and love.

Mrs. Long: Glad to hear you say it, Mrs. Todd. You know this is my first tea and I am so awkward in everything....

Mrs. Todd: Don't say that, dear Mrs. Long. You are perfectly at home in your place, and your tea is excellent. I guess I will have another cup of it.

Mrs. Long: You are welcome to as many as you like. Have some more cookies.

Mrs. Todd: Thank you very much. You certainly know how to entertain. And these cookies are just lovely. I know I will ask you for the formula some day.

Mrs. Long: They are the kind my mother bakes; we children always thought that there is nothing better.

Mrs. Todd: And I am certain, there isn't. They have such a fine delicate flavor and taste of love and appreciation. And what exquisite china you have! The pattern is plain and yet so tasteful and pleasing. I am sure I envy you. Oh, Mrs. Klock allow me to congratulate you on the great acquisition of another son to your family.

Mrs. Night: A son? What do you mean?

Mrs. Todd: I mean a son-in-law.

Mrs. Klock: Thank you.

Mrs. Night: A son-in-law! Is Milda to be married?

Mrs. Todd: Don't you know it, Mrs. Night? Miss Milda is engaged to Mr. George Robertson, the clerk in the city drug store.

Mrs. Night: What, to that grasshopper?

Mrs. Klock: Thank you for the compliment, Mrs. Night. I do well appreciate your kindly feelings, since your daughter Alma was after catching that grasshopper, as you delight in calling Mr. Robertson, but she didn't succeed.

Mrs. Night: Oh dear no! We are not in the least envious. If my daughter would want a man like Mr. Robertson, she wouldn't wait for him until she was 27 years old; she would pick him up in the first corner of an alley.

Mrs. Klock: Now, I'll leave. (*Rising angrily.*) This impertinence is more than I will stand.

Mrs. Night: Impertinence you call that? Allow me to return your compliment. It was impolite of you to intimate that my daughter was running after your Mr. Robertson.

Mrs. Klock: And it was shameful of you to call him a grasshopper.

Mrs. Todd: Ladies! Ladies! I must beg to spare me with a recital of your family troubles. You will do better to settle them between your own walls.

Mrs. Night: And you may stuff your ears if they are too tender for this.

Mrs. Klock: You flippy telltale are the cause of this racket. What made you begin it?

Mrs. Todd: My dear Mrs. Klock, was it wrong to congratulate you on your new son-in-law? I think not.

Mrs. Klock: Don't call me dear Mrs. Klock. It was your intention to brew trouble between me and Mrs. Night when you congratulated me.

Mrs. Todd: Indeed not! I meant what I said and how I said it.

Mrs. Night: Yes, we know how you said it! It was like a delicate stab with a barn fork right into the ribs.

Mrs. Todd: Dear me! Now they both are falling in on me. There, my dear Mrs. Long, take my cup and saucer and put it away. I must go.

Mrs. Klock: Yes, you better. There are some more people who don't know it; hurry and tell them.

Mrs. Todd: Now, my dear...ah, no!...Mrs. Klock you have no cause to say that to me.

Mrs. Long: Ladies! Ladies! I beg to remind you that this is my first afternoon tea.

Mrs. Klock: And what a mess you made of it!

Mrs. Long: Oh! Mrs. Klock! (*Turns away and weeps.*)

Mrs. Todd: (*Seeing that Mrs. Long weeps, embraces her.*) Don't weep, my dear, don't let this insult you. They do not mean it that harsh.

Mrs. Klock: No harm is meant, Mrs. Long, but I must go.

Mrs. Night: So must I.

Mrs. Klock: No, you stay back until I am outdoors. I don't want to be seen in your company. (*Exit.*)

Mrs. Night: You won't? Well, I'll see if the street isn't free for everybody. Goodby, Mrs. Long. Many thanks for your tea. (*Exit.*)

Mrs. Todd: Now they are gone. Turn around and be gay, Mrs. Long. (*Mrs. Long faces Mrs. Todd.*) Don't take them serious. Women often will say nasty things without meaning it.

Mrs. Long: Yes, they do mean it. They were in here before you came and I watched them through the door. They called my rug a rag carpet, and said that my china was semi-porcelain and that I hadn't any more china in the house than Mrs. Klock had on her head. They also tasted of my cookies and said that they were from the bakery. Oh, I can't tell you how ugly those women behaved.

Mrs. Todd: And now they punished themselves for their baseness. Really, Mrs. Long, I did not mean any harm when I congratulated her.

Mrs. Long: I believe you, I know you didn't, Mrs. Todd. But let that pass. I meant well for all of you when I invited you to my Five O'clock Tea, and how did they pay me back!

Mrs. Todd: We won't mind that, will we? But I know where the trouble came from. My dear Mrs. Long, now you must come to my Tea next Friday afternoon, will you?

Mrs. Long: I will try to come.

Mrs. Todd: No, you must promise for sure to be there and I promise you that nothing like this shall happen there. Take my word on it.

Mrs. Long: How can you promise that?

Mrs. Todd: I won't invite any mother-in-laws nor mothers with marriageable daughters, see?

Mrs. Long: (*Smilingly.*) All right, I'll be there.

Hot Chocolate

On winter days hot chocolate may have been offered in addition to tea. It was a popular drink for adults as well as children because it was mistakenly thought to be less stimulating than tea or coffee. In fact, so highly esteemed was the drink that porcelain figurines depicting women carrying trays of hot chocolate were popular decorative accessories for parlors. The hot chocolate that was consumed in Victorian times was not the same drink we make from powder-filled pouches today. Theirs was a much thicker and richer concoction that required preparation. Shavings from a grated block of chocolate had to be dissolved in boiling water. Milk was added and then heated until scalding. Other recipes called for the addition of two beaten egg yolks and sweetening with sugar. There were also those hostesses and cooks who preferred to roast their own cocoa shells, which they then ground into a paste. Boiling water was added to this paste, and the concoction boiled for another twenty minutes. Finally, boiling milk or cream and sugar was added, creating a drink similar to chocolate latte.

Chocolate pot; 10"h; Roses and ground color executed in overglaze paints; burnished gold handle and knob; Signed: "M. H. Dorothy"; Blank: GDA, France; ca. 1900-1941; $125-175.

Chocolate pot; 8½"h (missing lid); Delft-style scenes executed in overglaze paints, framed by acid-etched borders of roses and leaves; burnished gold borders, handle, spout, and base rim; Stamped: "White's Art Co., Chicago"; ca. 1914-1923; Blank: GDA, Limoges, France; $125-175.

Chocolate pot and two chocolate cups and saucers; chocolate pot, 9¼"h; Burnished gold knob, rims, handles, and base rims; Blank: Chocolate pot, Bavaria; ca. 1891-1914; cups and saucers, star, Limoges, France; ca. 1914-1920s; chocolate pot, $100-150; cups and saucers, $15-25.

Chocolate pot and stand; chocolate pot, 5¾"h; stand, 6⅝"dia; Burnished gold rims, spout, handle, knob, and stand; Blank: chocolate pot, T &V rectangle, Limoges, France; ca. 1892-1907; stand, wreath and star, R. S. Germany; ca. 1904-1938; chocolate pot, $65-95; stand, $15-25.

Chocolate cup and saucer; Primrose and ground color executed in overglaze paints; burnished gold rims, cup base, handle; Signed: "A. Brown"; Blank: Haviland, Limoges, France; ca. 1894-1931; $25-35.

Hershey's was the first manufacturer to package a mix of cocoa powder, sugar, and dried milk that only needed hot water added to make a drink of hot chocolate. This was in 1894. It would take more than three decades for its product to become popular.

Hot chocolate was served in special porcelain pots appropriately named chocolate pots. The French are credited with this invention that they called a *chocoliatiére*. Its form dates back to the end of the seventeenth century, but its roots can be traced back to Mexico before the time of Spanish conquest. The Spaniards improved the Mexican drink by covering the pot with a wooden lid that had a hole in the middle for a stirrer. Stirring created a frothy drink favored by the Spaniards. The French innovation was to attach a straight wooden handle at a right angle to the spout. This innovation was later applied to coffee pots as well. (See page 148.)

In Central America the Aztecs drank their chocolate drink cold or at room temperature, while the Europeans preferred their drink hot. Hot chocolate originally was consumed from small open bowls similar to early tea bowls. Cups and saucers were substituted for bowls in the seventeenth century to prevent the liquid from spilling on one's clothes. The first chocolate pots were made from silver, and later porcelain.

Porcelain chocolate sets, which consisted of the pot with its high spout and six cups and saucers, became fashionable during the 1880s and 1890s. A small serving of this drink did much to satisfy Victorian appetites. For most people, a 6-ounce serving sufficed. Some chocolate sets also included a sugar bowl and creamer, and a handled cookie tray. Like tea, hot chocolate was served on a tea table, which the hostess could set up adjacent to the fireplace for additional warmth.

Silhouettes & Spouts

What's the difference in silhouette between a teapot, a coffee pot, and a chocolate pot? Look at the profile and spout placement. In comparison, chocolate pots (top) are tall and narrow, as are the cups that accompany them. They also have a short, high spout. Sometimes there might be a small opening in the lid so that milk could be poured through this hole, and a muddler or miller (a long spoon) could be inserted for stirring.

Coffee pots also are tall, but are ovoid in shape. Their spout is connected closer to their base. Coffee grounds sink to the bottom and clean coffee is left in the rest of the pot. Teapots are more squat. Their shape makes allowances for the expansion of tea leaves which rise in hot water.

However, sometimes what might be considered a coffee pot is called a teapot. The reason for this is that these pots were used to serve iced tea—not hot tea (see Chapter 6).

Lemonade pitcher and lemonade cups; pitcher, 5¾"h; cups, 3½"h; Pitcher: blackberries and ground colors executed in overglaze paints; burnished gold handle; Signed: "C. N. Patterson, 1908"; Blank: J.P.L., France; $175-225; cups: currants, gooseberries, and ground colors executed in overglaze paints; burnished gold rims; Signed: "C. L., 1901"; Blank: none; $50-70.

Lemonade pitcher; 5¾"h; Grapes, border band, and ground colors executed in overglaze paints; Blank: none; ca. 1900-1918; $175-225.

Mug; 4¾"h; Gooseberries and ground colors executed in overglaze paints; Blank: crown, two shields, Vienna, Austria; ca. 1900-1915; $45-65.

Mug; 4¾"h; Grapes and ground colors executed in overglaze paints; burnished gold rim and handle; Blank: crown, two shields, Vienna, Austria; ca. 1905-1925; $50-75.

Set of four mugs; 3"h; Roses and ground colors executed in overglaze paints; burnished gold rim, handles and designs; Signed: "E. V. Ashley" and "E.V.A."; Blank: none; ca. 1900-1915; $60-80.

Set of four tumbler stands; 2¾"dia; Burnished gold rims, bright gold interiors; Blank: Epiag, Czechoslovakia; 1920-1939; $60-80.

Tumbler plate; 4½"dia; Burnished gold rim, band, and monogram; Stamped: "William Lycett, Atlanta"; ca. 1920-1938; $8-15.

Lemonade

On particularly hot days when lemons were in season, lemonade could be provided as a thirst quencher. Some lemonade pitchers had a bulbous shape, while others had tapered sides. Lemonade was poured into specially designed cups called tumblers, which often had handles so that individuals could hold the cup without warming the liquid, for the ice remained in the pitcher. Sets consisted of a pitcher, six tumblers, and a tray. Interestingly, lemonade sets were decorated with various fruits, flowers, and geometric designs, but rarely lemons!

Ambitious china painters also could purchase and decorate porcelain reamers with cups to catch the juice from squeezing lemons. Cautious hostesses were wise to provide porcelain coasters, known as tumbler stands, to protect wood surfaces.

Lemonade pitcher; 5¾"h; Conventional-style crab apples and ground color executed in overglaze paints; burnished gold rim, handle, and ground; Blank: none; ca. 1910-1920; $175-225.

What is the difference between a lemonade pitcher and a cider jug? Both liquids were poured from the same type of pitcher, and even the decoration does not provide a clue. For example, crab apples might be used as a decorative motif on either type of container. Mrs. C. C. Filkens, author of *The China Painters' A-B-C*, which was published in 1915, wrote, "Oranges, apples, crabapples, lemons and plums, are all suitable for large fruit bowls and lemonade pitchers." A few paragraphs later Filkens stated, "Crabapples for a cider jug are especially good . . ." Therefore, the container pictured above, which was decorated around the same time Filkens' book became available, could have been used to serve either lemonade or cider, depending on the season and the availability of the fruits.

Packing Punch

In eighteenth-century England, the consumption of alcohol, especially gin, was a common practice among all classes. Inexpensive raw spirits made from excess grain crops were readily available. The middle and upper classes, however, preferred rum imported from the West Indies, or French brandy. They mixed their alcohol with water or milk, lime or lemon juice, sugar, and spices to make a sweet punch. As the

The following recipe, which was printed in an unidentified newspaper, was found with dozens of other recipe clippings, some dated as late as 1918, in a cookbook published in 1894.

Japanese Punch

Boil together for five minutes one part of water, two pounds of sugar and the thin, yellow rind of two lemons. Strain, and add the juice of four lemons and one thinly sliced cucumber and let cool. When cool remove the cucumber and add two quarts of strong tea. Pour [liquids] over a block of ice in your punch bowl and add one pint of stoned cherries.

nineteenth century progressed, punch fell from its favored position as a common drink because of the resulting drunken state associated with its consumption.

Two types of punch were served in Victorian times: concoctions that included alcohol, and fruit drinks that did not. When callers came, the hostess might serve fruit punch as an alternative to tea or chocolate. Punch made with alcohol was reserved for special occasions.

In Georgian England, special bowls were used to serve punch, then transferred with a ladle to large, heavy glasses called rummers. Americans, however, preferred smaller cups. Porcelain punch sets included a large bowl, which might have a separate stand, twelve cups, and sometimes a ladle. Although punch may have been served in the parlor, these pieces usually were arranged on the sideboard in the dining room.

Punch bowl and stand; punch bowl, 9½"dia; Grapes, color band, and ground colors executed in overglaze paints; burnished gold rim and feet; Signed: "SANDWICH"; Blank: bowl, Favorite, Bavaria; ca. 1908-1918; stand: D & Co., Limoges, France; ca. 1905-1915; $350-450.

A similar porcelain blank was pictured in the Chicago-based china importer Burley & Tyrell's catalog number 19 (circa 1910), and listed as a salad bowl as well as a punch bowl. How can the finished piece be identified? In this example, by its fruit decoration, and by its stand, which a salad bowl would not have had.

Punch bowl; 10⅞"dia; Blackberries and ground colors executed in overglaze paints; mother-of-pearl luster blossoms inside rim; yellow luster interior; burnished gold rim, feet, and scrolling; Blank: T & V rectangle, Limoges, France; ca. 1892-1907; $800-1,200.

The August 1900 issue of *Keramic Studio* printed the following mottoes for china painters to use on punch bowls or steins.

Come here, my boy,
If you are dry,
The fault's in you
And not in I.

From mother earth I took my birth,
Then form'd a jug by man,
And now I stand here filled with
*   good cheer—*
Taste of me if you can.

Man wants but little here below
And wants that little strong.

Set of five punch cups; 4"h; Forget-me-nots executed in overglaze paints; mother-of-pearl luster interiors; burnished gold stems and rims; Blank: Royal wreath, O. & E. G.; 1898-1918; $105-120.

Set of two punch cups; 3"h; Conventional-style grape and geometric design executed in pale yellow and pink luster, matt paints, and burnished red gold; Blank: Royal wreath, O. & E. G.; 1898-1918; $50-70.

Parlors and the Pleasures of Idleness vs. Living Rooms

By the late 1800s, the parlor was metamorphosing into the modern living room. Change was apparent as one century slipped into the next, and priorities shifted from home entertainment to seeking pleasure elsewhere. As the number of servants diminished with each passing decade, while living spaces shrunk and women's work patterns changed, women were less willing to put forth the effort of intensive dusting and vacuuming required to maintain parlors.

With the passage of time the parlor's symbol as a repository of family aspirations faded. As early as 1881, Clarence Cook wrote in *The House Beautiful*, "I use the word 'Living-Room' instead of 'Parlor' because I am not intending to have anything to say about parlors. As these chapters are not written for rich people's reading, and as none but rich people can afford to have a room in their houses set apart for the pleasures of idleness, nothing would be gained by talking about such rooms."

Edward Bok, editor of *The Ladies' Home Journal* from 1889 to 1919, was another individual who inhaled the winds of change and presented the fresh ideas they brought as practical realities. He used the magazine to transform the common American home, beginning with the publication in 1895 of a series of modest houses in which either a living room or a library was substituted for a parlor—a room Bok, too, considered useless. Tens of thousands of plans sold, initiating the transformation. Later on, Sidney Morse, in his book *Household Discoveries*, reiterated Bok's sentiments: "The old custom of setting apart a 'best room' or parlor to be used only on special occasions . . . is happily passing away. Only very wealthy people now have drawing rooms reserved for state occasions. The present tendency is to call all the lower rooms of the house 'living rooms,' and to have all the members of the family use them freely."

Concurrently, the rise of the Arts and Crafts Movement, which favored function and simplicity over symbolism and ornateness, also mirrored changing sentiments. Society was transforming from one ruled by formalities, where social boundaries were distinct, to one of ease and intimacy, where conversations were less superficial and impersonal. The living rooms belonged as much to the man of the house as to its mistress. By 1920, the "living room" had usurped the "parlor," and all the porcelain bric-a-brac that once adorned the space.

*Drawing of a dining room from the November 1898 issue of **The Art Amateur**. (Photo credit: The Newberry Library, Chicago)*

"THE MOST SUITABLE FORM OF DINING-ROOM DECORATION
MUST OF NECESSITY BE THE CHINA OR SILVER
OF WHICH THE HOUSE MAY BOAST."

The House Beautiful, June 1898

Chapter Four

Dealing with Decoration: The Dining Room

Next to the parlor, the dining room held the greatest prestige. The opulence of this room symbolized the financial success, social status, and good taste of its owners. Families often started their day together in this room, and the serious business of entertaining took place here as well. Hosting a dinner party was a monthly endeavor and major social event.

Three-handled loving cup; 5¹¹⁄₁₆"dia by 6³⁄₈"h; Grapes and ground colors executed in overglaze paints; white enamel embellishments; burnished gold rim; Signed: "R. F. Chapman"; Blank: none; ca. 1900-1920; $175-225.

The dining table would be covered with felt or heavy flannel to protect its surface and to muffle sound. A heavy damask cloth that nearly reached the floor was placed on top. Flowers in a large porcelain vase, loving cup, or jardiniere provided the table decoration. "The decoration of the table is now one of the most important features of a luncheon or dinner party, and should receive the personal attention of the hostess," wrote Mrs. Grace Townsend in *Imperial Cook Book* (1894). "An elaborate display of flowers is not essential, as a few, if artistically arranged in attractive holders, will be just as beautiful and add as much to the elegant appearance of the table."

A new trend incorporating ferns and fern pots in the center of the dining table emerged in the mid-1890s. An article in the January 1896 edition of *The Ladies' Home Journal* discussed dainty china ferneries "filled with growing specimens of Nature's lace work," which formed the central table decoration in homes of taste and refinement. They were considered a vast improvement over the pyramids of fruit and flowers that overflowed from pedestal bowls, multi-tiered servers, and epergnes.

The writer considered the simplicity of low-laying fern pots artistically superior to the previous designs, which obscured guests seated across from each other.

The Victorians affiliated certain flowers and plants with specific meanings, using them to communicate silent messages. Ferns symbolized "sincerity," flowering ferns "fascination." Though more often associated with a bouquet a gentleman might present to a lady, fern-decorated porcelain spoke highly to honored guests. What better compliment could a person pay one's friends than to express the sincerity of their friendship, as well as to tell them how fascinating they found them?

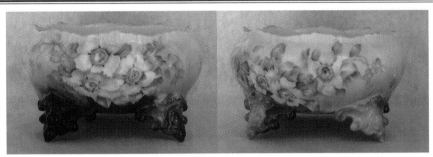

Fern pot; 7½"d by 4¾"h; Wild roses and ground colors executed in overglaze paints; Signed: "B E Miehling, 99" (1899); Stamped: Elite shield (Bawo & Dotter, New York City); Blank: Limoges, France; $150-200.

Fern pot with liner; 7⅝"dia by 4¾"h; Maidenhair ferns and ground colors executed in overglaze paints; white enamel embellishments; burnished gold rim and feet; Signed: "F. M. R., 1899"; Blank: France; $125-175.

Ferns also were used as a decorative motif on many kinds of porcelain. Not only were porcelain fern pots decorated with frothy fronds, but ferns appeared on tableware as well. For example, the leaf-shaped dish pictured on page 118 probably was used to serve pickles, which were routinely offered at lunch and dinner. The green of the plants and delicately shaded background would have nicely complemented the color of the pickles, while the gilding provided highlight and relief from the uniform color. Ferns also appear on the mustard pot pictured on page 105, and on the sandwich tray shown on page 117.

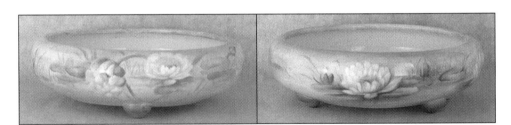

Lily bowl; 8"dia; Waterlilies and ground colors executed in overglaze paints; Signed: "E. B." Blank: Japan; ca. 1921-1930; $40-50.

Lily bowls were another type of low container. Waterlilies, which are found on numerous continents, have always been regarded as an exotic species because of their peculiar way of opening between certain hours, disappearing under water when closed—only to arise again at another time. They were ever popularized when the world's largest waterlily, with six-foot leaves, was discovered in British Guiana in 1837 and named "Victoria Regia" after Queen Victoria. This waterlily was brought to England to the estate of the Duke of Devonshire in Chatsworth.

When it first bloomed there in 1849, the event was well publicized, influencing designers and artists, as well as the general population.

The appeal of the waterlily as a design inspiration continued through one century and into the next, kindled by the craze for objects and decorations in the Japanese style of the 1870s and 1880s, and adapted as an Art Nouveau motif in the last decade of the nineteenth century and the first decade and a half of the twentieth.

Waterlily designs appeared on a variety of objects. These included a double-handled cake plate (see page 41), mustard pot (see page 106), cup and saucer (see page 49) and plates (see page 84), in addition to the lily bowl pictured here. In the language of flowers, waterlilies represented purity of heart.

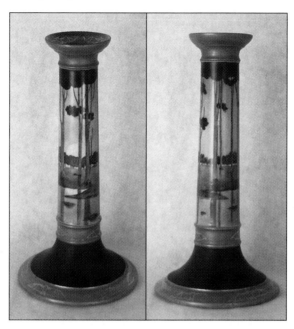

Candlestick; 7"h; Bands of roses executed in overglaze paints; burnished gold top, bottom rim, and banding; Signed: "C. M. Fritz"; Blank: none; ca. 1880–1900; $50–75.

Candlestick; 9"h; Landscape executed in overglaze paints; matt ground; gold borders incised with bats; Signed: "Olga Sorenson, '04"; Blank: Limoges scroll; $75–125.

Pair of candlesticks, 5¼"h; Ground and part of butterfly executed in matt paint; burnished gold butterfly wings and cups; Blank: Royal wreath, O. & E. G.; 1898–1918; $50–70.

Pair of candlesticks; 4½"h; Apple blossoms and ground colors executed in overglaze paints; burnished gold tops and bases; Blank: Royal wreath, O. & E. G.; 1898–1918; $50–70.

China closets date back to late seventeenth-century England, where storage and display of china were equally important. China was a prestigious possession. Those who owned expensive hand-painted pieces wanted to show them to advantage, while protecting them at the same time.

Candelabra and candlesticks flanked the centerpiece. Candlelight remained the fashionable form of lighting, even after electricity became available in urban dwellings in the 1890s. Neither gaslight nor electric light possessed the softness and romantic quality of shaded candlesticks. In the October 1901 issue of *Keramic Studio*, editor Adelaide Alsop Robineau described the following table setting: "A beautiful setting for a dinner table is to have a tall, single candlestick in front of each plate, with a tiny vase of flowers between; and a large loving cup or jardiniere filled with loose flowers in the centre of the table."

The sideboard, china closet, and fireplace mantel would be stocked with glittering displays of porcelain tableware and bric-a-brac, crystal, glass, and silver. Encircled by a plate rail, the room would be ringed with hand-painted examples. Large chargers (identified as chop plates in china catalogs) were either hung on walls, or placed on narrow bracketed shelves or on overmantel shelves, leaning against walls for support. The glimmer of reflective surfaces, patterned walls and window coverings, and decorative accessories, created a lavish background for social events. Such surroundings and accompanying formal, opulent dress provided enticing views throughout the dinner, which lasted as long as three hours.

Abundant food required abundant utensils, and each type of food had its own container. "Table china failed, until recently, to command the same attention as other branches of decorative arts," declared *The House Beautiful* magazine in their June 1898 issue. "Only the wealthy have been supposed to be interested in eating off pretty plates, and people with moderate means have been satisfied to use nondescript tablesets if they were free to have their diamond earrings and their sealskin sacques."

"Any one can have a lot of odds and ends collected at random, or the remnants of previous sets," wrote Mrs. Nicola de Rienzi Monachesi in *A Manual for China Painters*, "but to own a complete unbroken set of cups and saucers that have been decorated with a given and visible motive is decidedly more elegant and refined."

The sideboard was likely the most important innovation in American furniture of the Federal Period (1780-1830). Historians believe that it evolved from Robert Adam, a popular British architect of the mid-eighteenth century who is said to have placed knife boxes (to show off the family silver) flanked by urn-shaped wine coolers at opposite ends of a serving table. Often there was a shelf below the tabletop for plates or dessert. By the end of the nineteenth century, the large, elaborately-carved sideboard was the most important piece of dining room furniture. It was as symbolic as it was practical, storing porcelain, silver, and crystal, or as a place to serve drinks and food.

What constituted a complete set? In the article "Decoration of a Table Service," which appeared in the March 1892 edition of *The Art Amateur*, the author suggested that six soup plates, six dinner plates, and 18 breakfast plates were sufficient for a family of six, for the additional breakfast plates could be used as part of a five-course dinner to serve fish, salad, and dessert. Three meat dishes in graduating sizes (the medium-size to be used for the entrée), a salad bowl, ice cream dish, and sauce boat were necessary accessories. Additionally, if the ice cream dish was scored with a grid pattern, it could be used as an asparagus set, along with the sauce boat and breakfast plates.

China distributors offered sets in addition to open stock pieces. For example, Burley & Company listed a 100-piece dinner set in their catalog number 70 (ca. 1910). It consisted of the following items:

Chop plate; 14¼"dia; Roses and ground colors executed in overglaze paints; Signed: "L.R.P., Jan. 1900"; Blank: D & Co., Limoges, France; $450-550.

Chargers originally referred to large round or oval-shaped dishes that were used as meat platters. They were at least 12 inches wide. By the late Victorian era, chargers, which were called chop plates in china catalogs, were more likely to be used decoratively, rather than used as tableware.

> 12 dinner plates
> 12 tea plates
> 12 soup plates
> 12 sauce plates (probably fruit saucers)
> 12 individual butters
> 1 large, 1 medium, and 1 small platter
> 1 open vegetable dish
> 1 soup tureen
> 1 sauce boat
> 2 pickles
> 1 covered butter
> 12 tea cups and saucers

About twenty years later, distributors such as the Maurer-Campana Art Co., were still selling similar 100-piece dinner sets in their August 1, 1929, catalog.

An editorial in the December 1914 issue of *Keramic Studio* listed the "correct" diameters for plates. Measurements were made from the outside edge on one side to the inside rim on the other, "according to trade practices;" the overall measurement would be "quite a little more," as Robineau, its editor, wrote:

fish, 7½ inches
game, 7½ inches
fruit, 6½ inches
salad, 7½ inches, though 6½ inches often used
service plates, 8½ to 9 inches
dinner plates, 8½ inches
breakfast plates, 7½ inches
supper plates, 6½ inches
dessert, 6½ inches

Twenty-five years later, dining habits had changed, and with it, so did tableware. *The American Woman's Cook Book*, published in 1940, listed the following sizes for various plates, less numerous than in previous decades:

place plate or service plate, 10 to 11 inches
dinner plate, 10 to 10½ inches
entrée plate, 8½ to 9½ inches
dessert plate, 7½ to 8 inches
bread and butter plate, 6 to 6½ inches
soup plate, 8 to 8½ inches

The size of the dinner plate became larger to accommodate the placement of vegetables, since these were no longer served separately. The entrée plate doubled as a salad or fish plate, and even as a dessert plate. Likewise, the dessert plate also could be used as a salad plate, while at tea it became the cake plate. As meals simplified and people streamlined their lifestyles, tableware became less specialized and more adaptable.

A Matter of Course

The focal point of the dining room was definitely the fully set table. Individual place settings, called covers, included many other pieces of tableware, glassware, silverware, and napkins. Twenty-five to thirty inches were allowed for each cover during the late 1800s; by the 1920s, twenty to twenty-four inches was sufficient since the number of courses and requisite silverware and glassware had diminished. Whatever the size allowance, covers were expected to be placed with mathematical precision.

The service plate, whose purpose was decorative rather than functional, was placed in the center. It usually was an inch larger than the dinner plate, averaging 10 to 12 inches in diameter, and more ornate than the rest of the china. However, food was never served on this plate. Instead, the plate for the first course would be placed upon it. The service plate would remain in place until the last course before dessert. The bread and butter plate, or pat, when employed, was located first to the right of the service plate and above the knife, and later to the left, replaced by individual nut dishes on the right. An individual salt dip with spoon also was placed to the left, although salt and pepper shakers were placed above the service plate in line with the glasses, or between two covers.

Napkin rings were invented in 1867. They were intended for family use only, unless a guest was staying with the family for some time. Since washing was done on a weekly basis, linen napkins were reused for several meals. According to Maud C. Cooke in *Our Deportment*, ". . . unless fresh napkins are supplied at every meal, they should be folded and placed in the napkin ring." "Napkins are never supposed to appear a second time

Napkin ring; 2"dia; Forget-me-nots and ground colors executed in overglaze paints; white enamel embellishments; burnished gold rims; Blank: none; Signed: "Luken" (Minnie A. Luken, Luken Art Studios, Chicago, 1895-1926); $15-25.

Napkin ring; 2½"w; Columbine and ground color executed in overglaze paints; Blank: none; ca. 1880-1915; $10-20.

without washing," stated Mrs. Townsend in *Imperial Cook Book*. "Hence, napkin rings are domestic secrets, and not for company." (Paper napkins first appeared in England in 1887; the only reference to their use in American publications is at children's parties.) Water pitchers were placed between every two or three guests. Additional porcelain pieces used throughout the meal were dependent upon the menu.

While many cookbooks and etiquette books of the Victorian time period cover extensively the type of wine and liquor offered with particular dinner courses, family dinners of the middle class likely included beer, if they included alcohol at all.

Stein; 5⅛"h; Gaggle of geese in a forest landscape executed in overglaze paints; Signed: "Cora Wright" (New York City, ca. 1897-1907); Blank: T & V rectangle; $75-95.

Stein; 5"h; Strawberry design and ground colors executed in overglaze paints; burnished gold rim and dragon handle; Signed: "Mabel Carlson, 1917"; Blank: crown, H & Co., Selb, Bavaria; $75-95.

What was the difference between a beer stein and a beer mug? Steins held fifteen, thirty, or ninety fluid ounces of beer. Mugs usually held only twelve ounces of the drink.

Beer Basics

For many people, beer was consumed at a typical family meal, rather than offered at a formal dinner. While inebriating, it was considered a thirst quencher and food accompaniment, imbibed as we do soft drinks today. This was during a time period when water remained suspect as to its purity, and often rightly so. When settlers began brewing beer in this country, their brew was similar to English and Dutch beers. These beers were of the ale family, brewed with top-fermenting yeast made from barley malt. The drawback to this type of brewing was its instability and the way the yeast in the brews picked up wild yeasts in the air, turning the beer bitter.

Early immigrants consumed beer from black leather jugs called "black-jacks." Seventeenth-century New Yorkers preferred pewter tankards, with glass replacing pewter as the material of choice just prior to the American Revolution. The preference for porcelain probably arose with the influx of German immigrants beginning around 1850.

These immigrants transformed American brewing methods with their introduction of lager beer. It was brewed with a heavy, bottom-fermented yeast that was not exposed to air. This yielded a better, more stable brew.

Lager beer quickly became popular. In 1850 there were 431 breweries in the United States producing around 750,000 barrels of beer a year. A decade later the number of breweries had almost tripled, producing over a million barrels of beer annually; and by 1880 over 13 million barrels of beer were consumed. Ten years later, beer accounted for half the alcohol consumed in America.

"The souvenir spoon, the teapot, the jug, and the teacup collector, while still pursuing their several ways with more or less ardor, are likely to be eclipsed this season by the beer-mug fad. Six medium-sized mugs ranged about a larger one is the usual arrangement, and the very least that one possessed with the craze can get along with . . . Some of these mugs have metal lids, while others are guiltless of any attempt at concealment of their contents."

Crockery & Glass Journal, *March 1899*

Left: Stein; 5"h; Blackberries and ground colors executed in overglaze paints; burnished gold rims, border band, and handle; Signed: "France Studio" (Robert W. France, Chicago, 1906-1916); Blank: crown, crossed scepters, Rosenthal, Bavaria; $85-105. Right: Tankard; 12"h; Cherries and ground colors executed in overglaze paints; burnished gold rim, handle, and base bands; Signed: "C. Heyn" (Charles Heyn), "France Studio" (Chicago, ca. 1906-1916); $250-325.

"The collecting of drinking vessels has much more to excuse its existence than that of the vast majority of objects which have recently become the game of the omnipresent collectors. A fine collection of such vessels, when out of service, not only serves to decorate a dining room and to play an eminently practical part in the festivities of the house, but often repays careful examination, exhibiting such a range of ma(n)ufacture, material and decoration, as to be of more than passing interest as one phase of artisanship."

The House Beautiful
June 1897

Miniature ewer vase; 4½"h; Forget-me-nots and ground colors executed in overglaze paints; burnished gold handle and rim; Signed: "Wollaston"; Blank: Royal wreath, O. & E. G., Austria; 1898-1918; $25-30.

Matches cruet pictured on page 108.

A single flower or miniature bouquet might be placed beside each cover, or in a bud vase, for the ladies as well as the gentlemen. "Nothing imparts such an inviting appearance to a table as flowers," wrote Mrs. Townsend in *Imperial Cook Book*. "When flowers are plentiful, not only should the center pieces be filled with them, but a small bunch tastefully arranged should be placed before each guest, those for the gentlemen being composed only of a few leaves and a blossom or two." The flowers became a souvenir for the ladies, while the men placed theirs in their buttonholes.

Napkins were folded into a rectangular shape and laid upon the center of each plate, or to the left of the forks. A small piece of bread or roll was placed on top of, or partially within, the folds of the napkin. A name card could be either on top of the napkin or over the service plate.

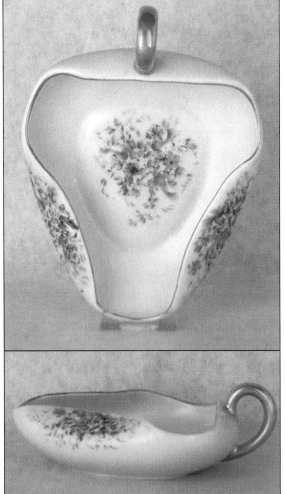

Double-handled, footed bonbon bowl; 5½"dia; Roses and ground colors executed in overglaze paints; burnished gold rim, handles, and feet; Blank: none; ca. 1900-1925; $45-55.

Ring-handled bonbon dish; 6"w by 4¾"d; Forget-me-nots and ground colors executed in overglaze paints; white enamel embellishments; burnished gold rim and handle; Signed: "E. Q."; Blank: Bavaria; ca. 1891-1914; $20-35.

Double-handled bonbon bowl; 6"sq; Burnished gold rim, handles, foot; Blank: none; ca. 1920-1930; $35-45.

To balance the composition of a table, decorative dishes for bonbons or nuts were placed at the corners of the table. "Nuts are ordinarily served only at dinner," stated Maria Willett Howard, author of *Lowney's Cook Book*, a tradition that likely reached back centuries.

Nuts, which could be found in all parts of the country, could be gathered during nutting trips in the fall, which often made for a fun outing. "Off they go with bright, laughing eyes and glowing cheeks, each one carrying a light little basket or fancy bag slung carelessly on her arm. The girls are full of life and spirits as they walk briskly along toward the woods in the delightful fall weather, talking and laughing in a happy, thoughtless fashion, now telling where the best nuts are to be found . . . ," wrote sisters Lina and Adelia B. Beard in *The American Girls Handy Book*, originally published in 1887. Hickory nuts, black walnuts, butternuts, and hazelnuts were found in abundance, as were chestnuts before the blight in the early 1900s. Then, too, treats such as California walnuts and Brazil nuts also could be offered.

Nut bowl; 7"dia; Chestnuts and ground colors executed in overglaze paints; mother-of-pearl luster interior; burnished gold rim; Blank: Royal wreath, O. & E. G. Austria; 1898–1918; $50–65.

Nut bowl; 5½"dia; Acorns and ground colors executed in overglaze paints; yellow luster interior; Signed: "A. Mueller, '07; Blank: none; $25–45.

Boat nut bowl; 5½"w by 4½"d by 2⅝"h; Gooseberries and ground colors executed in overglaze paints; burnished gold rim; Signed: "STONER"; Blank: Favorite, Bavaria; ca. 1908–1918; $25–45.

Almonds, pecans, filberts, peanuts, and walnuts could be cracked and a portion of the shell discarded, or they could be blanched and salted. These were served in porcelain nut bowls, which commonly had sensuous, bulbous shapes and undulating rims rolling inward. Decorations varied from acorns and pine cones in nut-like earth tones to florals that matched the dinnerware.

At Your Service

There were three ways to serve meals: the English, the Russian, and the Compromise service. No matter which service was utilized, ladies always were served first, beginning with the guest of honor seated to the right of the host.

The English style of serving was similar to what is known as family style today. In any given course, all the food to be served was placed on platters or in proper containers on the table at the same time. The required number of plates was piled near the host. After carving the meat, each plate received is portion and was carried by a waiter or waitress, or by the host, hostess, or some other family member, to the person who was serving another type of food, such as vegetables, before finally placing it before a guest. This method was particularly suited to households with limited help.

The Russian style of service was the most formal. With the exception of nuts, candy, and relishes, no other food appeared on the table. Each plate either was filled in the pantry and brought directly to a guest, or aesthetically arranged platters of food were offered by the servant and guests helped themselves, filling their empty plates.

The Compromise service was a combination of the English and Russian styles. For example, soup could be served Russian-style, while the meat course could be served English-style. For most middle class families, this style of service was typical.

"Since food is ornamental in itself it is more attractive when served on dishes that are not overdecorated. Conventional patterns in china are therefore to be preferred to all-over floral designs."

Everyday Foods, Jessie W. Harris and Elisabeth V. Lacey, 1927

Left: *Individual berry bowl; 6⅝"dia; Nasturtiums executed in overglaze paints; burnished gold border and rim. Signed: "H. B. F." Blank: CFH/GDM, 1870-1882; $15-25.* **Right:** *Plate; 8½"dia; Conventional-style nasturtiums and ground color executed in overglaze paints; burnished gold rim; Blank: H & Co., Limoges, France; ca. 1888-1896; $35-45.*

Naturalistic designs depicted motifs in a realistic manner. In contrast, the conventional style reinterpreted natural forms geometrically, or used basic geometric forms to create motifs.

When the china painting movement began in 1876, naturalism was the reigning style. Conventional designs began appearing during the mid-1880s, gaining ground as the Arts and Crafts Movement and Art Nouveau style spread throughout the United States. By the mid-teens, the conventional style was viewed as modern, preferable to the naturalistic style, which by then appeared old-fashioned.

However, many china painters continued to paint in a naturalistic manner in spite of prevailing trends, for there remained those who found comfort in the traditional.

Plates for Service, Plates for Display

Plate; 8½"dia; Apples and ground colors executed in overglaze paints; burnished gold rim; Signed: "S. Heap" (Samuel Heap); Stamped: "Stouffer" (Stouffer Studio, Chicago, 1906–1914); Blank: J.P.L., France; $65–85.

Plate; 8¼"dia; Plums and ground colors executed in overglaze paints; burnished gold rim; Blank: crown, shield, and wreath, Bavaria; ca. 1903+; $25–35.

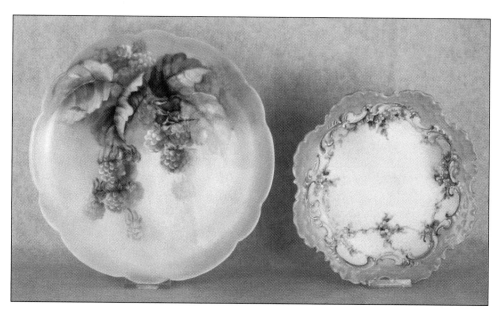

Left: *Plate; 8¾"dia; Raspberries and ground colors executed in overglaze paints; white enamel embellishments; Signed: "Arkwright" (attributed to Blanche Arkwright, Council Bluffs, Iowa, ca. 1906); Blank: France; ca. 1891–1914; $35–50.* **Right:** *Plate; 6¾"dia; Forget-me-nots and ground colors executed in overglaze paints; white enamel embellishments; Signed: "Arkwright" (attributed to Blanche Arkwright, Council Bluffs, Iowa, ca. 1906); Blank: crown, crossed scepters, R. C., Monbijou, Bavaria; $20–30.*

Plate; 7⅝"dia; Pansies and ground colors executed in overglaze paints; Signed: "L.V.W. 1903"; Blank: crown, crossed scepters, R.C., Bavaria; $25-35.

Plate; 8¼"dia; Wild roses and ground colors executed in overglaze paints; enameled and burnished gold scrolling; burnished gold rim; Blank: T & V rectangle, France; ca. 1892-1907; $35-50.

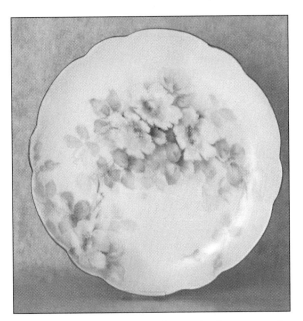

Plate; 8½"dia; Wild roses and ground colors executed in overglaze paints; burnished gold rim; Importers mark: "G. H. B. Co."; Blank: J & C, Bavaria; ca. 1911; $25-45.

Plate; 9½"dia; Daisies and ground color executed in overglaze paints; burnished gold rim, scroll, and inner band; Signed: "LCR"; Blank: T & V rectangle, Limoges, France; ca. 1892-1907; $45-65.

Plate; 9¼"dia; Magnolia and ground color executed in matt paints; burnished gold scrolls, details, and rim; Blank: T & V rectangle, Limoges, France; ca. 1892-1907; $45-65.

Plate; 8"dia; Orchids, maidenhair ferns, and ground color executed in overglaze paints; white enamel highlights; burnished gold rim, scrolls, and feathering; Signed: "F. C. Rhodes, 4-98"; Blank: MR, France; $35-50.

Plate; 7½"dia; Tulips and ground color executed in overglaze paints; burnished gold outlines, border band, and rim; Signed: "Wight"; Blank: crown, H & Co., Selb, Bavaria; 1911-1934; $25-40.

Plate; 8¼"dia; Poppies executed in overglaze paints; burnished gold decorations and rim; Blank: France; ca. 1891-1914; $35-45.

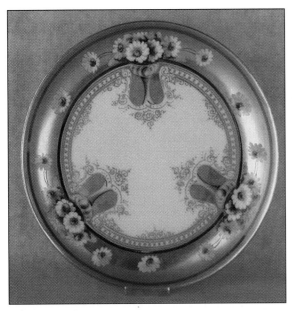

Plate; 8½"dia; Daisies and urns executed in overglaze paints; burnished gold borders, bands, scrolls, and rim; Stamped: "Stouffer" (Stouffer Studio, Chicago, 1906-1914); Blank: Haviland, France; $45-65.

Plate; 8½"dia; Conventional-style lilies and borders executed in platinum and burnished gold; Signed: "Kind" Stamped: "Stouffer" (Stouffer Studio, Chicago, 1906-1914); Blank: Haviland, France; $45-65.

Plate; 8½"dia; Roses and ground colors executed in overglaze paints; burnished gold rim; Signed: "F. B. Betts"; Blank: Haviland, France; 1894-1931; $35-50.

Plate; 8¼"dia; Roses and ground colors executed in overglaze paints; burnished gold rim; Blank: T & V rectangle, Limoges, France; ca. 1892-1907; $35-50.

Plate; 9¼"dia; Geraniums executed in overglaze paints; white enamel embellishments; burnished gold rim; Signed: "Mrs. Moore" Blank: T & V rectangle, Limoges, France; ca. 1892-1907; $35-50.

Plate; 7½"dia; Stylized bird, cherry blossoms, and ground colors executed in overglaze paints; Signed: "Musselman" Blank: Royal wreath, O. & E. G., Austria; 1898-1918; $18-25.

Plate; 8⅜"dia; Peacocks, landscape, feathers, and butterflies executed in overglaze paints; burnished gold border and rim; Blank: Leonard, Vienna; ca. 1890s; $35-50.

Plate; 8⅝"dia; Butterflies executed in overglaze paints and luster; burnished gold spider web; Signed: "M. Wigginton"; Blank: crowned double-headed bird, MZ, Austria; ca. 1900; $35-50.

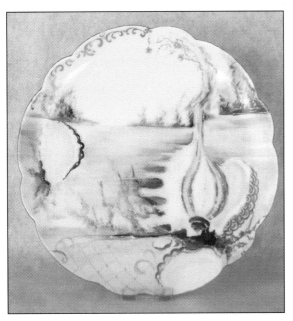

Plate; 8⅜"dia; Seashells, seaweeds, and water executed in overglaze paints; white enamel embellishments; burnished gold decorations and rim; Signed: "A. M. N."; Blank: H & Co., Limoges, France; ca. 1876-1879; $35-50.

Plate; 9½"dia; Maple leaves and ground colors executed in overglaze paints; burnished gold rim; Signed: "Brentwood"; Blank: D & Co., Limoges, France; ca. 1894-1900; $35-50.

Plate; 7⅞"dia; Beechnuts and ground colors executed in overglaze paints; burnished gold rim; Signed: "L. M. T."; Blank: crown, crossed scepters, Rosenthal, Selb, Bavaria; ca. 1908-1925; $25-45.

The major difference between plates meant to hold food and plates meant for decoration is in the placement of the design. Border designs were considered more appropriate for tableware, where the pattern would remain in view throughout a meal and be less subject to damage from cutlery. "The mistaken china painter who splashes big flowers over her plates, to be messed up in gravy and garnished with pickles—or who paints dainty cupids to be drowned in soup, is decidedly absent-minded, to speak in mild terms," wrote Robineau in the March 1904 edition of *Keramic Studio*.

Plate; 7¼"dia; Peppers executed in overglaze paints; burnished gold rim; Signed: "Mill. S"; Blank: T & V rectangle, Limoges, France; ca. 1892-1907; $18-25.

"While we are sighing for novelties and new worlds to conquer, suppose we take a walk around the vegetable garden one of these fine mornings. We may gain something by going to this humble source for models for the decoration of our table service with little fear that association will rob them of their beauty.

"Some of the small varieties of Peppers, scarlet and orange, are very ornamental, as good as a flower."

"Suggestions From the Kitchen Garden"
by C. E. Brady
The Art Amateur, *July 1896*

Plate; 6¾"dia; Roses executed in overglaze paints; burnished gold rim and border; Signed: "Denison"; Blank: Thomas shield, Sevres, Bavaria; ca. 1908; $10-20.

Plate; 8¼"dia; Roses and border band executed in overglaze paints; Blank: row of buildings or crown, Silesia; ca. 1915; $25-35.

Plate; 6½"dia; Roses and ground color executed in overglaze paints; mother-of-pearl luster band; burnished gold borders and rim; Blank: Thomas shield, Bavaria; ca. 1908; $15-35.

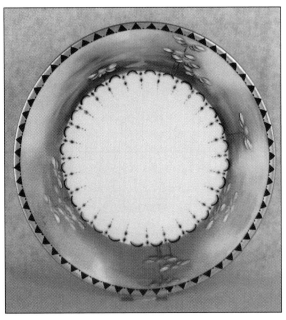

Plate; 8½"dia; Conventional-style daisies and ground colors executed in overglaze paints; matt paint border details; burnished gold rim and inner border; Signed: "C. M. (McMiller?); Talladega, Ala."; Blank: B & Co., France; ca. 1900-1914; $35-50.

Plate; 7½"dia; Roses and ground colors executed in overglaze paints; burnished gold rim; Signed: "Kayser" (Mrs. Magdalena Kayser, Milwaukee, ca. 1910-1915); Blank: Favorite, Bavaria; $25-40.

Plate; 7½"dia; Conventional-style waterlilies and ground colors executed in overglaze paints; burnished gold borders and rim; Blank: J & C, Bavaria; ca. 1902; $18-30.

Plate; 8¾"dia; Conventional-style waterlilies and ground color executed in overglaze paints; burnished gold rim; Blank: Thomas shield, Sevres, Bavaria; ca. 1908; $25-40.

Plate; 8⁵/₁₆"dia; Stylized design of violets and ground color executed in overglaze paints; Signed: "Seybold" Blank: none; ca. 1906-1916; $25-40.

Plate; 8¼"dia; Daffodils and ground colors executed in overglaze paints; white enamel embellishments; burnished gold rim; Blank: Thomas shield, Bavaria; ca. 1908; $25-40.

Plate; 8½"dia; Daisies, border band, and ground colors executed in overglaze paints; burnished gold rim and bands; Signed: "Blake"; Stamped: "Rogers-Martini Co." (Chicago, 1913-1916); Blank: T & V rectangle, Limoges, France; $35-50.

Plate; 8½"dia; Poppies and border colors executed in overglaze paints; burnished gold rim and scrolls; Signed: "W. Stupe"; Blank: Thomas shield, Bavaria; ca. 1908; $35-50.

Plate; 7⅝"dia; Conventional-style acorns, oak leaves, and ground colors executed in overglaze paints; burnished gold rim; Signed: "J. Townsend"; Blank: Hutschenreuther, Bavaria; ca. 1887; $18-25.

Plate; 7¾"dia; Conventional-style birds and ground colors executed in overglaze paints; burnished gold rim; Blank: circle and rectangle, Bassett Limoges, Austria; ca. 1909-1915; $18-30.

Plate; 7⅝"dia; Conventional-style peacock, tree, background, and border executed in overglaze paints; burnished gold "leaves;" Signed: "Painted by Grace P. Merwin, Indianapolis"; Blank: Thomas shield, Sevres, Bavaria; ca. 1908; $20-30.

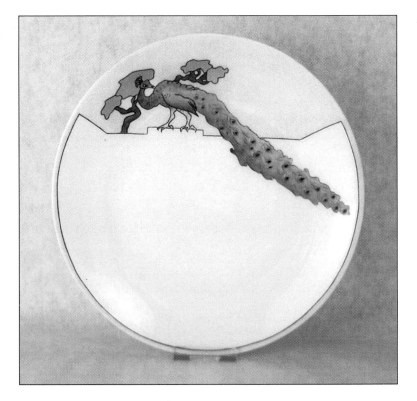

Plate; 8½"dia; Fans, cherry blossoms, and border ground color executed in overglaze paints; burnished gold border; Signed: "Mamie Stuber" Blank: Thomas shield, Sevres, Bavaria; ca. 1908; $35-50.

There were exceptions, of course. Dessert services, which always were the most ornate as a grand finale to a meal, might feature floral compositions strewn across the surfaces. Game plates, too, depicted birds and animals in landscape settings over their central portions. Bear in mind that the latter types of plates often doubled as decoration when not in use. They made beautiful accents on sideboards and in china closets—pieces of furniture that often cost more than the dining table and reflected the family's wealth and refinement.

"Nothing reveals the individual more than the taste displayed in the decoration of table china, whether it shows the tendency for the practical, for the artistic or for the overloaded," wrote Robineau in the March 1902 editorial of *Keramic Studio*. Whether simple or ornate, naturalistic or conventional, porcelains were decorated to appeal to a plethora of tastes and desires.

"CONDIMENTS ARE ... USED TO STIMULATE THE APPETITE
BY ADDING FLAVOR TO FOOD."

—Fannie Merritt Farmer
The Boston Cooking-School Cook Book, 1896

Chapter Five

Condiments and Compliments: Food Flavorings

ondiments spiced up and sweetened relatively bland Victorian foods. Many of these condiments were stored in decorative porcelain containers that added elegant touches to Victorian table settings. People used sugar shakers to sweeten fruits or desserts, cruet bottles for vinegar and oil salad dressings. Syrup pitchers, gravy boats, sauce bowls, mustard pots, and jam jars also held their respective condiments.

Spun, Nipped or Spooned, Sugar Has Remained the Choice Sweetener

For at least three thousand years, honey collected from wild bees was the chief sweetener. It wasn't until the thirteenth century that sugar began to replace honey as a major sweetener in wealthy European households. Over time, sugar's use increased proportionally with the rise in consumption of tea and coffee.

When sugar became more readily available in Europe in the sixteenth century, Italian confectioners became known for the intricacy of their spun-sugar sculptures. It had long been a European custom among the wealthy to adorn their banquet tables at dessert with elaborate buildings, gardens, and figures made from sugar.

With the advent of porcelain, the popularity of porcelain figurines replaced sugar shapes by the mid-eighteenth century. Porcelain, though even more expensive than sugar, was more durable. Pieces could be rearranged at every banquet. However, in Colonial America, wealthy colonists still decorated Twelfth Night cakes, baked for the "Twelfth Night" party at the end of the Christmas season, with edible sugar figures that formed a ring on top of the cakes.

Yet throughout the nineteenth century sugar remained an expensive commodity. This was partly because in North America sugar was an imported product, originating in the West Indies. (It was Columbus who introduced sugarcane to the Caribbean from Brazil.) Factored into this import cost was the time and expense involved in processing raw sugar.

Raw sugar, which required four separate stages to manufacture, was packed into cone-shaped clay molds that drew off molasses syrup from the sugar crystals. One sugar cone could weigh up to ten pounds and last up to a year if used sparingly. These cones came wrapped in deep blue-violet colored paper to make the sugar, which had a yellow cast, appear whiter. This paper was saved and soaked for its dye to color textiles.

Brown sugar, which was tinted by traces of molasses, was reserved for cooking, while white sugar, which was more expensive, was used at the table. For the latter, whiteness and fineness of texture were prized. It also was less subject to spoiling, since it contained less nutrients that supported bacterial growth.

Sugar and creamer; Stylized rose design executed in overglaze paints; mother-of-pearl luster bands, knob and handles; Blank: KPM, Silesia, Germany; ca. 1904-1927; $30-40.

Sugar and creamer; Roses and ground colors executed in overglaze paints; burnished gold borders, rims, base rims, and handles; Blank: creamer, bird, C. T. Altwasser, Silesia; sugar, KPM; ca. 1909-1930; $30-40.

Sugar and creamer; Conventional-style floral design executed in colored enamels; burnished gold borders, rims, and handle; Blank: Favorite, Bavaria; ca. 1908-1918; $30-40.

Sugar bowl; 2"h; Roses and border band executed in overglaze paints; burnished gold borders and handles; Signed: "Claire White"; Blank: bird, C. T., Altwasser, Germany; ca. 1909-1934; $15-25.

Covered sugar bowl; 3½"h; Roses and ground colors executed in overglaze paints, burnished gold rims; Blank: star, wreath, R. S. Germany; ca. 1904-1938; $15-25.

Matches gravy boat with attached stand pictured on page 138.

Creamer; 3"h; Poppies and ground color executed in overglaze paints; mother-of-pearl luster interior; burnished gold border, rim and handle; Blank: KPM, Germany; ca. 1904-1927; $15-25.

Creamer; 2¾"h; Conventional-style roses and ground colors executed in overglaze paints; burnished gold border, rims, and handle; Signed: "G. Sitz"; Blank: wreath and star, R. S. Germany; ca. 1904-1938; $15-25.

Creamer; 3½"h; Forget-me-nots and ground colors executed in overglaze paints; white enamel highlights; burnished gold rim and handle; Signed: "Brown"; Blank: none; ca. 1910-1920; $10-20.

Creamer; 4½"h; Light blue and yellow ground executed in overglaze paints; burnished gold borders, rim, handle, and monogram; Blank: Royal wreath, O. & E. G., Austria; 1898-1918; $15-25.

Creamer; 2⅝"h; Oranges and border band executed in overglaze paints; burnished gold rim and handle; Blank: Crown over oval encircling PL, Imperial, Austria; ca. 1914-1918; $10-20.

Small lumps were cut from cones with a cleaver and with sugar nips, and placed in porcelain sugar bowls on tea trays. Sugar tongs were used to transfer lumps to individual tea cups. It was exacting work to cut pieces of equal size and regular shape, a task considered too delicate and too important to be entrusted to servants.

"In pouring coffee, the sugar and cream are placed in the cup first. For tea it is better to pour first, and then add cream and sugar."

—*Imperial Cook Book,*
MRS. GRACE TOWNSEND, 1894

Consequently, wives and daughters were responsible for performing this delicate operation.

The process of sugar refining took over three weeks to complete. In 1868, Claus Spreckels of San Francisco patented a method of sugar refinery that required only eight hours. The vacuum pan, used in conjunction with a centrifuge, revolutionized sugar processing. Spreckels' invention, coupled with the lifting of sugar tariffs in the 1880s, resulted in a great price drop for sugar, making it affordable for most people.

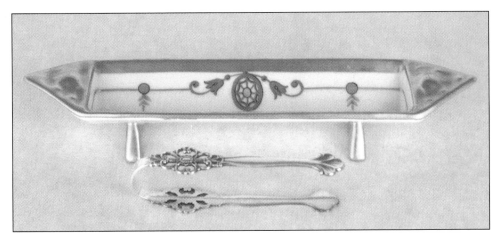

Loaf sugar tray, shown with sugar cube tongs; 8"w by 1½"d by 1¼"h; Design executed in overglaze paints; burnished gold designs, rim, and feet; Decorated in Pickard China Company's "Adam Border"; Stamped: "W.A. Pickard, Hand Painted China"; ca. 1912-1918; Blank: none; $100-125.

Henry Tate of London patented a device that cut sugar loaves into small, regular-shaped and sized pieces. These were first produced in 1878 and proved to be so popular that Tate amassed a fortune within a short time. Today, sugar cubes are made by mixing white crystals with pure white syrup, then molding to the desired shape.

Cubed sugar was first served in sugar bowls, and later in specially designed troughs called loaf sugar holders, loaf sugar trays, or simply sugar trays.

Sugar shakers, or sugars, as the porcelain pieces were commonly called, came into use in the last quarter of the nineteenth century. They were used for scattering caster sugar—a fine type of sugar resembling powdered sugar—and later cinnamon, over cake or fruit. The tops on these pieces were domed and perforated with large holes. They held about a cup of sugar. The use of sugar shakers were common until around 1910, when their employment dwindled in the mid-teens, ironically just as the consumption of white sugar reached an all-time high. This trend quickly reversed when sugar became a rationed food at the time the United States entered World War I in 1917.

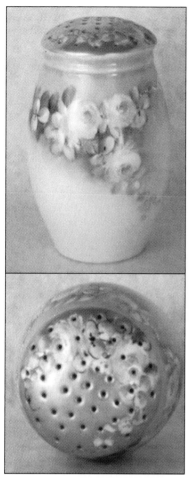

Sugar shaker; 4½"h; Roses and ground colors executed in overglaze paints; burnished gold top; Signed: "E. W. Lawer, B29"; Blank: none; ca. 1900-1930; $50-75.

Sugar shaker; 4½"h; Burnished gold conventional floral design and top; Signed: "E. C. R."; Blank: none; ca. 1905-1915; $25-45.

Worth Its Salt

Salt is so taken for granted that we forget how precious this essential mineral once was. At one time, salt was used as a form of money, and coins were even made from salt. The word "salary" dates back to a time when Roman soldiers received part of their compensation in the form of salt. The salt trade was so profitable that almost all countries had a salt tax, right into the twentieth century! Since prehistoric times, people collected salt from the sea. Numerous salt mines were discovered in the nineteenth century, making this element more plentiful and less expensive, although still invaluable.

Used as a seasoning as well as a preservative, something as important and precious as salt dictated that it have its own special container on the dining table. In the latter half of the seventeenth century, as separate dining rooms and individual place settings at the dining table were gaining in popularity, elaborate standing salt boxes were being replaced by simpler saltcellars.

Salt dip; 3"dia; Flowers and colored panels executed in overglaze paints; burnished gold rim and scrolls; Signed: "L. J. G."; Blank: none; 1890-1910; $25-35.

Set of six salt dips; 1⅝"dia; Forget-me-nots and ground color executed in overglaze paints; burnished gold rims and feet; Blank: none; ca. 1892-1907; $60-90.

Matches butter tub pictured on page 99, signed "Tossy."

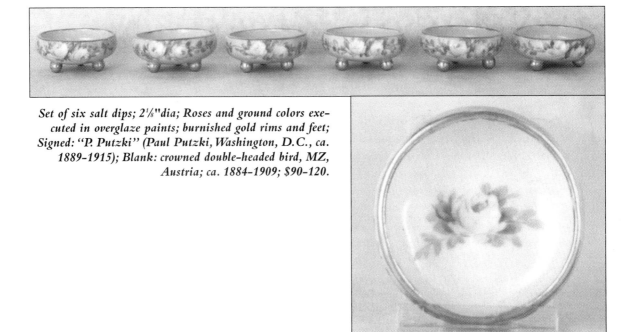

Set of six salt dips; 2⅛"dia; Roses and ground colors executed in overglaze paints; burnished gold rims and feet; Signed: "P. Putzki" (Paul Putzki, Washington, D.C., ca. 1889-1915); Blank: crowned double-headed bird, MZ, Austria; ca. 1884-1909; $90-120.

Salt dip; 2¾"dia; Roses, forget-me-nots, and ground color executed in overglaze paints; burnished gold rims; Blank: Royal wreath, O. & E.G., Austria; ca. 1898–1918; $40–80.

Salt dip; 2¾"dia; Forget-me-nots and ground color executed in overglaze paints; raised paste and burnished gold scrolls, lattice, and dots; burnished gold interior border, feet, and rim; Blank: T & V rectangle, Limoges, France; ca. 1892–1907; $20–30.

The cauldron-shaped salt dip was the most popular shape. Its form was also used for individual bonbon dishes, nut dishes, olive dishes, and berry bowls, all differentiated by size. Bonbon, nut, and olive dishes measured from 3½ to 5 inches in diameter. Berry bowls measured 6 to 7½ inches in diameter.

Initially called trenchers, these were square or polygonal-shaped boxes. Some had lids, and some were divided to hold a second condiment. This form was succeeded by lidless saltcellars which were shaped like spools. Over time the most common and popular shape was the shorter cauldron, a round or oval bowl supported on three legs. These saltcellars first appeared in the eighteenth century, continuing production into the early part of this century. They were made from silver, porcelain, ceramic, and glass.

This small serving piece, identified as individual salts, salt dips, or celery dips (for dipping celery stalks) in china catalogs, became a required part of dining etiquette. According to *Buckeye Cookery and Practical Housekeeping* (1880), "Individual salt-dishes are used at breakfasts, but not at dinners—a cruet, with salt dish and spoon, at each end of the table, being preferred as giving the table less of a hotel air." About ten years later, beginning in the 1890s, individual salt dips were placed at the top left-hand side of the dinner plate, or between every other person.

Diners used small salt spoons to scoop some salt onto the rim of the dinner plate. Victorians, who considered it vulgar to have one's fingers touch their food, felt that by using these small spoons, a feeling of delicacy and propriety was preserved when serving from a common bowl, to say nothing of potential contamination. Additionally, this practice insured that salt, which was still somewhat expensive, would be conserved.

Hand-painted porcelain salt dips and salt and pepper shakers are highly collectible. Despite their small size, salt dips can carry a high price tag. They range from as low as $15 to as high as $40. On the other hand, a single salt shaker (without a cork stopper) may sell for as little as $5, and a pair for as much as $40, depending on the decoration and, at times, the manufacturer.

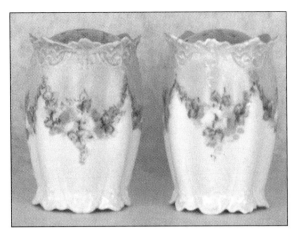

Salt and pepper shakers; 2⅞"h; Roses and ground color executed in overglaze paints; burnished gold tops; Signed: "Luman"; Blank: none; ca. 1900-1920; $20-30.

Salt and pepper shakers; 3"h; Roses, forget-me-nots, and ground colors executed in overglaze paints; Blank: none; ca. 1900-1920; $20-30.

Salt and pepper shakers; 2½"h; Line design and ground color executed in overglaze paints; burnished gold borders, neck bands, and tops; Blank: none; ca. 1910-1930; $15-22.

Salt (3"h) and pepper (2½"h) shakers; Dogbane and ground colors executed in overglaze paint; burnished gold tops; Signed: "A. W. McGarry, Cincinnati, Ohio" (Amy W. McGarry, 1897-1933); Blank: none; $25-35.

Salt and pepper shakers; 3"h; Oranges and ground colors executed in overglaze paints; burnished gold bands; Signed: "H. B. Hill, Saratoga, N.Y." (Hazel B. Hill, 1908-1915); Blank: Royal wreath, O. & E.G., Austria; $25-35.

Salt or pepper shaker; 2⅞"h; Conventional-style cherry blossom design and ground color executed in overglaze paints; burnished gold top; Blank: Bavaria; ca. 1891-1914; $10-15.

Salt or pepper shaker; 2½"h; Bands of ground color executed in overglaze paints; burnished gold top, bands, and monogram; Signed: "E. KUMSTEAD"; Blank: none; ca. 1900-1920; $10-15.

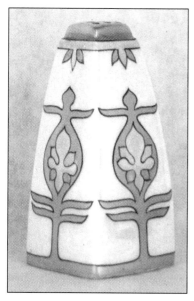

Salt or pepper shaker; Conventional design in luster, enamel, burnished gold; Signed: (Margaret) "Carlyle, St. Paul, Minn."; Blank: Germany; ca. 1891-1914; $10-15.

Double or combination salt and pepper; 2¼"h; Roses and ground color executed in overglaze paints; burnished gold bands, handle, rim, and tops; Blank: none; ca. 1900-1920; $15-25.

Serving salt from a salt dip was not always practical. Many must have found it difficult to evenly distribute salt on their food. On September 15, 1863, a patent for a salt and pepper shaker as we know them today was granted. Originally this item was called a salt and pepper dredge. According to Webster's *New World Dictionary*, the word "dredge" has two meanings, and the second applies to this item. As a verb transitive, dredge means to sprinkle.

However, on damp and rainy days, salt would cake, making it difficult to use. Morton International, Inc., producers of Morton© brand table salt, and to this day the major salt supplier in the United States, found a solution to this dilemma. In 1914, a team of their researchers developed a purified salt containing an additive of magnesium carbonate that allowed the salt to freely flow in any weather. With this development, salt shakers gained in popularity, eventually replacing salt dips.

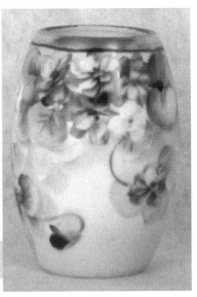

Three-piece condiment set (missing tray); Forget-me-nots and ground colors executed in overglaze paints; white enamel accents; burnished gold rim and tops; Signed: "E. Grech"; Blank: Germany; ca. 1891-1914; $40-50.

Toothpick holder; 2¾"h; Double violets executed in overglaze paints; burnished gold rim; Signed: "Wats" and "Pitkin & Brooks Studio" (Chicago, 1903-1910); Blank: T & V rectangle, Limoges, France; $20-28.

Some salt and pepper sets included toothpick holders. Toothpick holders were a common item, and toothpicks were frequently employed despite protests from etiquette advisors. Most of these experts agreed on one thing: Never pick your teeth at the table.

Buttering Up

In the Victorian era, butter remained a precious commodity because of its expense and perishability. Factory production of butter, which began in the United States in 1861, streamlined processing methods. However, it remained a perishable product. As with other luxury food items, butter's status required that it be featured on the table in special containers.

Butter was shaped in round wooden molds called "butter prints." One-pound cakes usually measuring four inches in diameter were made from these molds.

Porcelain tubs with 5-inch diameters took their shape and size from the one-pound butter cakes. Only after 1900 was creamery butter readily available. It was first cut into quarter-pound bars by Land O'Lakes in 1922. It took more than five years for rectangular porcelain butter dishes to be offered to the china painting market.

Butter tub; 4⅞"dia (missing perforated insert and possibly plate); Forget-me-nots and ground color executed in overglaze paints; burnished gold rim and handles; Signed: "Tossy"; Blank: T & V rectangle, Limoges, France; ca. 1892-1917; $35-55.

Matches salt dips pictured on page 94. This blank also was shown as an ice tub and bonbon dish in china catalogs. The bonbon dish came with a matching cover and no plate. Ice and butter tubs sometimes came with plates and had perforated inserts.

A butter tub set consisted of three- or four-pieces, including the tub, a perforated insert that allowed whey, which oozed from homemade butter, to drain through, a cover, and sometimes a plate. Even though ice boxes were in common use by 1838, and the first domestic refrigerator was developed in Chicago in 1913, most people did not refrigerate butter. Salt was used to improve flavor and act as a preservative, albeit one with a short shelf-life. Butter remained perishable and precious.

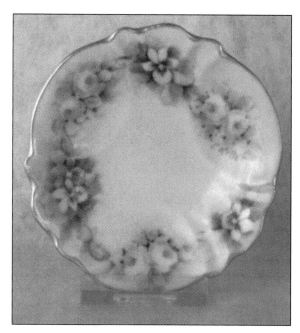

Individual butter dish; 3"dia; Roses, violets and ground color executed in overglaze paints; burnished gold rim; Signed: "E. Keller"; Blank: Shields, Schwarzenhammer, Bavaria Bermany; ca. 1905-present; $10-20.

Individual butter dish; 2⅝"sq; Forget-me-nots and ground color executed in overglaze paints; burnished gold rim; Signed: "E. Keller"; Blank: H & Co., Haviland, France; ca. 1876-1879; $10-20.

Set of six individual butter dishes; 2½"sq; Various plants, landscapes, and bird executed in overglaze paints; burnished gold rims; Blank: CFH, Charles Field Haviland, Limoges, France; ca. 1868-1881; $60-90.

Butter tubs appeared at meals and at tea time to be spread on warm cakes and bread. Individual butter plates, chips, pats, or pads, as identified in various catalogs, were employed. At family breakfasts, individual butter pats were "placed near the point of the knife," according to Maud C. Cooke, author of *Our Deportment, or the Manners and Customs of Polite Society*. Decorative butter swirls, rolls or pattern-stamped pats would be placed on each person's butter pat. As an alternative, butter-balls could be served from a small, 6- to 7-inch diameter ring-handled dish called a "butterball tray." Since each diner was either doled out an individual portion, or offered servings in pre-measured portions, no one overindulged.

Bread and butter plate; 6"dia; Conventional design executed in overglaze paints; burnished gold border and rim; Stamped: "F. Kastner, Milwaukee" (1912-1916); Blank: Hutschenreuther, Selb, Bavaria; $15-20.

Bread and butter plate; 6⅛"dia; Conventional-style design of wild roses executed in overglaze paints, with burnished gold details; burnished gold rim; Signed: "Yeazel"; Blank: Imperial crown, PSL, Empire I in oval; 1914-1918; $15-25.

*Bread and butter plate; 6"dia;Wild roses and ground
colors executed in overglaze paints; burnished gold
rim; Signed: "Belle Steele"; Blank: none; ca. 1900-
1920; $15-25.*

*Bread and butter plate; 6"dia; Roses, border band, and
ground color executed in overglaze paints; burnished
gold rim; Signed: "Laughlin"; Blank: Crown, crossed
scepters, Titanic; ca. 1890-1910; $18-25.*

*Bread and butter plate; 6⅛"dia; Roses and ground
color executed in overglaze paints; burnished gold rim
and medallion frames; Signed: (illegible); Blank:
Haviland, France; ca. 1894-1931; $18-25.*

*Bread and butter plate; 6"dia;Yellow roses and ground
color executed in overglaze paints; burnished gold
scrolls and rim; Signed: "Kreis" (Carrie S. Kreis,
Marion, Ohio, ca. 1901-1918); Blank: crown, crossed
scepters, Gotham, Austria; $15-25.*

Bread and butter plate; 6"dia; Currants and ground colors executed in overglaze paints; burnished gold border and rim; Signed: "Wands" (William D. Wands, Chicago, 1910-1916); Blank: UNO-IT, Favorite, Bavaria; $15-$25.

Bread and butter plate; 6"d; Cherries and ground colors executed in overglaze paints; burnished gold rim; Signed: "Louis F."; Stamped: "Keates Art Studios, Chicago" (1920-1937); Blank: Favorite, Bavaria; $15-20.

Bread and butter plate; 6"dia; Cherries and border band executed in overglaze paints; burnished gold rim and border bands; Signed: "Pep"; Blank: J & C, Bavaria; ca. 1902; $10-18.

Bread and butter plates were not included with dinnerware until the 1890s, although they were used at tea time. Initially a dinner roll was enclosed within a folded napkin set at each place. "Bread eaten with meat should not be buttered. Bread and butter is a dish for dessert," admonished the author of *Buckeye Cookery*. In the May 1899 issue of *The Art Interchange*, it was stated that bread and butter plates were only to be used for breakfast and lunch; "butter has no place on the dinner table, and the usual tiny butter plate must be omitted. . ." However, the March 23, 1899, issue of the *Crockery & Glass Journal*, offered a conflicting opinion.

"More than a year ago it was authoritatively announced that bread and butter plates were going out. But they have not gone. In fact, dealers are selling more of them to day than ever before . . .

"The bread and butter plate was too dainty a bit of table furnishing to part with, and too convenient. The hostess clings to it because it solves a problem in table setting; and the guest appreciates it because it solves a question in manipulation. So that a woman may still use bread and butter plates with the knowledge that she is entirely abreast of the times, and she may offer them as a wedding gift and be certain they will be appreciated."

The number of bread and butter plates that are scattered throughout the antique marketplace attests to the validity of the latter's opinion. The bread and butter plate, which measured from four to six inches in diameter, was placed first to the right, then to the left of, and above, the place plate. Bread or rolls were broken into small mouthfuls and buttered with a small butter knife as each piece was eaten.

The use of butter in the United States peaked during the 1920s and 1930s. In the 1940s, margarine began replacing butter because it cost less and was available, while butter was rationed after the United States entered World War II in 1941, until the war ended in 1945. As time passed, concern about cholesterol and fat consumption insured margarine's preference. Bread and butter plates eventually replaced butter pats, except at fashionable restaurants and hotels, where they prevailed until the 1940s. Butter pats and tubs became quaint dining paraphernalia.

Mustard Pots and Mayonnaise

Our ancestors discovered that sauces not only enhanced meat, fish, and poultry, but also disguised less than palatable entrées. By the eighteenth century, sauces

Mustard was first manufactured in this country by Benjamin Jackson in Philadelphia. He sold his product in glass bottles, and advertised in the February 15, 1768 edition of the PENNSYLVANIA CHRONICLE *that he was "the original establisher of the mustard manufactory in America…"*

were such an established and appreciated part of food culture that sauce-making guilds were organized in France.

Mayonnaise, a mixture of egg yolks, oil, lemon juice or vinegar, and seasonings, was introduced in America around 1800. Originally considered a delicate and exotic creation, it became an essential ingredient in many kinds of salads and salad dressings. Sauces and mayonnaise were served from dishes with an average diameter of 5½ inches. Mustard and jams were served from lidded pots with a small opening in their covers for a spoon.

Mayonnaise bowl (4½"dia) and plate (5⁷⁄₁₆"dia); Forget-me-nots and ground colors executed in overglaze paints; burnished gold rims and feet; Signed: "AG"; Stamped: "Stouffer" (Stouffer Studio, Chicago, 1906-1914); $18-30.

Also listed as a whip cream set in china catalogs.

Mayonnaise bowl (3⅝"dia) and plate (5"dia); burnished gold rims; Blank: P. P., Limoges, France; ca. 1903-1917; $18-30.

Mayonnaise bowl with attached plate; 5⅝"dia; Conventional design executed in overglaze paints, with colored enamel details; burnished gold borders and rims; Signed: "E. H. Hall"; Blank: Haviland, France; ca. 1894-1931; $18-30.

Mayonnaise boat and plate; 6"w; burnished gold interior, rims, handle, and monogram; Blank: wreath and star, R. S. Germany; ca. 1904-1938; $15-35.

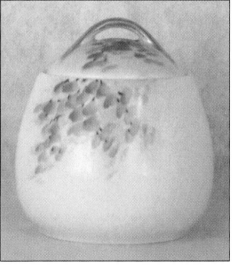

Mustard pot with spoon; 3"h; Maidenhair ferns executed in overglaze paints; burnished gold handles; Signed: "E. M. B. S."; Blank: wreath and star, R. S. Germany; ca. 1904-1938; $35-45.

Mustard pot with spoon; 2½"h; Burnished gold rims, knob, handle, and spoon; Blank: wreath and star, R. S. Germany; ca. 1904–1938; $35–50.

Mustard pot with spoon and plate; 3½"h; Conventional design executed in overglaze paints and burnished gold; burnished gold rims and knob; Signed: "E. L. H."; Blank: wreath and scepter, R. S., Germany; ca. 1904–1938; $45–65.

Mustard pot with attached plate; 3"h; Conventional-style waterlily design and ground color executed in over-glaze paints; burnished gold borders and handle; Blank: D & Co., France; ca. 1879–1900; $35–45.

What is the difference between a mustard pot, jam jar, and jelly jar? Jelly jars are taller. Jam jars are wider. Mustard pots, which may or may not have a single handle, are the smallest of the three. The lids of jam jars and mustard pots have a cutout for a serving spoon; jelly jar lids do not. Some jelly jars had a hole in their base. Jellies were one type of food offered in tin cans. This hole allowed a person to push up the can without having to turn the container over. Since mustard and home-made jams were placed directly into their pots, a hole would have been a messy inconvenience!

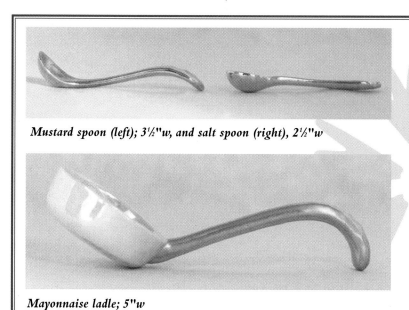

Mustard spoon (left); 3½"w, and salt spoon (right), 2½"w

Mayonnaise ladle; 5"w

Various condiments required different serving pieces as well. What was the difference between mustard, salt, and mayonnaise spoons and ladles? Size and shape account for the differences. Mustard spoons have S-shaped handles, while salt spoons have straight handles. Mayonnaise ladles also are straight, curving at the tip. Their bowls are wider and deeper.

Cruets

Caster sets are believed to have developed from frames designed in the late eighteenth century for holding glass oil and vinegar cruets and other condiments, although there is evidence that their basic design is a derivative of the oil and water cruets used during church Masses as early as 1720. Caster sets became a quintessentially Victorian item, popular from around 1840 onwards. Usually made from glass and silver, caster sets could include cruet bottles, a pair of salt and pepper shakers, mustard pot, jars for chutney, and even egg cups, bouquet holders, and a bell for summoning servants.

They were prominently placed in the center of most middle class Victorian dinner tables. (When not in use, they were stored on the sideboard.) As their popularity increased, these sets became taller and their designs more elaborate to reflect their status.

According to Mrs. Isabella Beeton, author of *Mrs. Beaton's Book of Household Management* (1861), condiments were required to prevent raw vegetables from "fermenting on the stomach." Habits once formed, no matter how obsolete the original reasons become, are rarely broken. Additionally, diners discovered the taste enhancement dressings and condiments provided.

Cruet with stopper; 6½"h; Forget-me-nots and ground colors executed in overglaze paints; burnished gold rim, inside lip, handle, and stopper; Blank: Royal wreath, O. & E. G., Austria, ca. 1899-1918; $60-80.

From set signed "Wollaston"; matches miniature ewer pictured on page 73.

Cruet; 6½"h; Mayflowers and ground colors executed in overglaze paints; burnished gold rim, inside lip, handle, and stopper; Signed: "R. A. S."; Blank: Oepiag, Czechoslovakia; ca. 1920-1935; $60-80.

Cruets, which comprised the main part of caster sets, were one-handled, narrow-necked bottles shaped like small decanters and sealed with a stopper. (Ewers, which are similar to cruets, have wider necks and no stopper.) They ranged in size from around 6½ to 8 inches high. Depending on shape and size, cruets held anywhere from eight to twelve ounces of liquid. Though more commonly made from glass, porcelain importers offered cruet blanks that china painters could embellish to their liking.

Cruets were often made in pairs, one for oil and one for vinegar. "Where salads are dressed at the table," wrote Fannie Merritt Farmer in *The Boston Cooking-School Cook Book*, "first sprinkle with salt and pepper, add oil, and lastly vinegar. If vinegar is added before oil, the greens will become wet, and oil will not cling, but settle to bottom of bowl."

How does one decide whether a piece of porcelain is a cruet or a cologne bottle? Some china catalogs offered perfume bottles in the same shape as cruet bottles. The difference between the two depended upon the size. Perfume bottles varied from 4 to as much as 6 inches in height; cruets measured 6½ or more inches high.

Casters diminished in size and significance on dining tables beginning in the 1890s. "The castor, too, is banished from tables polite, and its place may be taken by a few flowers, or bits of vine, in a simple vase. . . . Fancy sauce and vinegar cruets, and salts and peppers are grouped at each end of the table, sometimes on small trays . . .," wrote author Maud C. Cooke. Fruit dishes, centerpieces, and berry bowls also appeared with increasing frequency. By around 1900, condiment sets, which were smaller and less prominent, replaced castor sets. Fashions in table decoration had changed. Although diners still employed castor sets, people desired table centerpieces that were artistic rather than functional.

"SOME HAVE TABLEWARE DECORATED TO MATCH THE
COLORS OF THE DINING-ROOM, OR SETS OF DIFFERENT
PATTERNS FOR EACH COURSE..."

Buckeye Cookery and Practical Housekeeping, 1880

Chapter Six

Breakfast and Lunch

Beginning with Breakfast

The number of porcelain pieces employed at breakfast was a matter of choice, ranging from simply a tea or coffee pot, cream and sugar with cup and saucer and plate, to the very elaborate set including egg cup, cereal bowl, grapefruit plate, muffin dish, jam pot, and pitchers for both cream and hot water. For most people, a pot for coffee, sugar and cream, egg cup and cereal bowl, with plate, cup and saucer, and an extra plate for toast, were quite sufficient.

Two-piece toast or breakfast set; plate, 9³⁄₁₆"w; Conventional-style strawberries and ground color executed in overglaze paints; mother-of-pearl luster cup interior; burnished gold borders, rims, and handle; Blank: none; ca. 1925–1930; $35–50.

Also listed as a sandwich set in some china catalogs.

Covered muffin dish; 9¼"dia; Apple blossoms and ground colors executed in overglaze paints; burnished gold rim and handle; Signed: "E. Starer"; Blank: J & C, "Louise," Bavaria; ca. 1902; $250–325.

Covered butter dishes in the same shape were pictured in china catalogs. (Some even had a hole in the lid near the handle in similar fashion to covered muffin tops.) Size determined the function of the piece. Covered butter dishes ranged from 7 to 8 inches in diameter. They also had a separate perforated insert to allow whey to ooze through.

The following breakfast set was described in the May 1913 edition of *The House Beautiful*.

"A most complete and artistic set is comprised of a muffin or hot toast dish which has a cover, a small plate, cereal bowl and cream pitcher . . . a sugar bowl, egg cup, cup and saucer, fruit plate, and small coffee pot. These are . . . painted on white French china with a conventionalized apple and leaf motif, carried out in gray green and red enamels."

Four piece condiment set; tray, 7⅜"w by 4½"d; salt and pepper shakers; toothpick holder; poppy border executed in overglaze paints; burnished gold rims and tops; Blank: Germany; ca. 1891-1914; $45-55.

Jelly jar; 3¼"dia by 4⅞"h; Roses and ground colors executed in overglaze paints; burnished gold rims, knob, and foot; Blank: none; ca. 1905-1920; $30-50.

Jelly jar; 3¼"dia by 4⅛"h; (Missing lid and plate); Raspberries executed in overglaze paints; burnished gold rim; Blank: Lenox wreath, Trenton, N.J.; ca. 1906-1930; $25-35.

Jam or marmalade jar; 4¼"dia by 4½"h; Conventional-style fruit design executed in overglaze paints; burnished gold band and handle; Blank: wavy line, Z. S. & Co., Bavaria; ca. 1880; $30-50.

Fruit was preserved in various ways for use throughout the year. Jelly was made from fruit juice, sugar, and pectic or gelatin. Jam was made from fresh or dried fruit, rather than juice. Marmalade was a form of thick jam, made from the pulp and the juice of fruits, and containing pieces of fruit. Preserves contained whole fruits rather than pieces.

A caster containing a combination of pieces, such as a salt and pepper shaker, cruet, jam pot, and even a toothpick holder, was placed in the center of the table. Fruit was served first, followed by hot or cold cereal, eggs, meat (usually chicken or duck) or fish, potatoes, some type of bread or muffins, then hot cakes served with honey or maple syrup and coffee or cocoa.

Oatmeal was initially used as a gruel for invalids. It was purchased in an apothecary shop instead of a grocery store. Changes in production methods resulted in a consistent, tastier, and less gooey product, establishing oatmeal as a breakfast staple beginning in 1875. However, many still associated oats with animal fodder, of which it was a chief component, and it took some time before oatmeal became an acceptable breakfast food for the masses.

Cereal bowl; 7½"dia; Daisies and ground colors executed in overglaze paints; burnished gold rim; Blank: Circle, HR, Hutschenreuther, Selb, Bavaria; ca. 1905-1918; $15-30.

Milk or cream pitcher; 3⅜"h; and plate, 5¼"dia; Conventional-style orange blossoms executed in overglaze paints; burnished gold borders, rims, spout, and handle; Signed: "J. M. Cliffe, 11/28"; Blank: Japan; $25-35.

The nineteenth century also witnessed the invention and acceptance of prepackaged dry cereal. Two factors were directly responsible for this trend. One was that people had become more sedentary in their work and habits as a result of the Industrial Revolution. The large, high-fat, high-energy breakfasts that once sustained those who physically labored all day were unnecessary for those who worked in factories or at desks. Secondly, as more people worked outside the home, they had less time to linger in the morning. They wanted something to eat that was quick and light. Shredded Wheat was the first manufactured cereal, created in 1893, but other cereals that followed also gained wide appeal.

Some people were concerned with healthier lifestyles, and they believed a vegetarian diet to be superior. Dr. John H. Kellogg at the Battle Creek Sanitarium in Michigan was one such individual who prescribed a strict vegetarian regime for his patients. Kellogg developed a dry, ready-to-eat corn flake cereal in 1895 in response to a patient's complaint that the hardened cracker he ordered for her breakfast had broken a tooth. So popular was this type of cereal that by 1912 there were more than one hundred different brands of corn flakes!

Charles William Post was a patient of Kellogg's who eventually became his rival. Post was so enamored with breakfast cereal that he invented his own, beginning with Grape Nuts in 1897. Two years later it was being distributed in Canada and Great Britian, and the cereal competition escalated from there. Pre-packaged, ready-to-eat breakfast cereals—convenient, quick, and consistent in quality—lead to their widespread acceptance by the general population.

Butter was served in small tubs. Honey or maple syrup for hot cakes and hot biscuits were served in dishes, though maple syrup also could be poured from a syrup jug.

Eggs remained the breakfast food of choice for many Victorians, a tradition going back at least two thousand years. "When we consider that nine eggs are equal in nutritive value to a pound of meat, we realize they are not only capable of forming a most important item in everyday diet, but also an economical food during the season when eggs are cheap," stated Isabel Gordon Curtis in her *Mrs. Curtis's Cook Book.* Whether living on farms or in bucolic suburbs, many people raised their own chickens (along with vegetables and fruits in kitchen gardens). Boiled, fried, scrambled, baked, or poached—eggs were one of the least expensive breakfast foods.

Eating an egg from its shell required a special holder because of its peculiar, ovoid shape. The creation of the egg cup, then, was a matter of necessity, but the exact date and place where egg cups were developed has not been discovered. The earliest known examples, made of silver, were unearthed from the ruins of Pompeii. Romans were using these, then, prior to 79 A.D. The earliest existing ceramic egg cups are Spanish, and date from around 1630 to 1650. Another cup made from soft-paste porcelain was manufactured by the French St. Cloud factory in 1690. These were followed by the English factories of Chelsea in 1750 and Bow in 1760. The first hard-paste porcelain egg cups did not appear until Meissen manufactured them in the mid-eighteenth century.

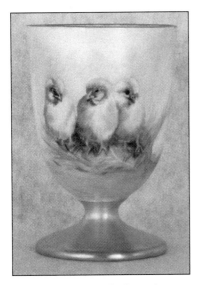

Egg cup; 3½"h; Chicks and ground colors executed in overglaze paints; burnished gold rim and base; Signed: "M. L. Hicok"; Blank: none; ca. 1920-1960; $35-55.

Pair of single egg cups; 3"h; Roses and border bands executed in overglaze paints; burnished gold rims; Blank: T & V rectangle, Limoges, France; ca. 1892-1907; $50-75.

Set of six double egg cups; 3⅜"h; Daisies and ground colors executed in overglaze paints; burnished gold rims; Blank: none; ca. 1890-1920; $90-125.

Early egg cups were single egg cups. Whether roasted or boiled, egg cups allowed one to eat the egg out of the shell. Double egg cups provided the option of being able to remove the egg from the shell and eat it from the larger end, where salt, pepper, butter, or toast could be added. This end also accommodated larger eggs, such as duck and goose. Exactly when or by whom the double egg cup was invented is unknown, but by the 1880s, most Americans preferred the double egg cup because of its versatility.

Sticky Sweeteners: Maple Syrup

For buckwheat cakes or waffles, maple syrup was an essential condiment. Maple sugar and maple syrup are unique to North America. In Colonial times, maple sugar was the most reliable source of sweetener and a necessity for the isolated farmer in America and Canada. Maple syrup was used in making a variety of dishes. It also could be used as a substitute for molasses.

Maple trees needed no cultivation, for they were self-seeding and self-perpetuating. They grew in the Northeast, around the Great Lakes and the St. Lawrence River, as far south as Virginia, and as far west as Minnesota, Iowa, and Missouri, as well as in Quebec and Ontario, Canada. While sugar plantations relied on slave labor for production, maple sugaring did not.

We are indebted to the native North Americans for maple sugar (as well as for pancakes), for it was they who taught European settlers how to tap trees, collect the sap, and boil it. The American Revolution forced a greater self-reliance on the colonists, and maple sugaring became a required skill. Cane sugar had to be imported from the West Indies, while maple syrup and sugar came from their own backyards.

As early as 1812, however, white cane sugar was gaining favor. It was available in general stores, in small towns, and served at inns. White cane sugar was expensive. For this reason, it was coveted, used sparingly, and limited to special occasions.

The development of improved equipment and sugar processing, coupled with the removal of tariffs, cut the price of cane sugar. By the early 1880s, cane and maple sugar equalized in price.

Syrup jug; 4"h (missing plate); Roses and ground color executed in overglaze paints; mother-of-pearl luster inside spout; burnished gold handle, knob, border, and rim; Blank: ADK, France; ca. 1891-1910; $25-35.

By 1885, cane sugar was less expensive than maple sugar, forever diminishing the latter's mass appeal. Consider, too, that it took about thirty-five gallons of boiled sap to produce one gallon of maple syrup.

The Victorian era was an age of specialization where each food item had its own utensils, and jugs for maple syrup were no exception. It also was an age with a philosophical bend that cried out for the combination of aesthetics and utility. Food was not served in its store packaging. Even an item as common as maple syrup, offered at breakfast, the least formal meal, could be dressed up in pretty florals.

Today, "real" maple syrup is considered a delicacy, while cane sugar is common. In fact, most commercially-made maple syrups only contain a small amount of true maple syrup—cane sugar syrup and corn syrup being the main ingredients. Maple trees are still tapped in the Northeastern part of the United States and are also appreciated for the shade they provide in summer, and the brilliant colored leaves they produce in autumn.

Lunch Bunch

Luncheons, like afternoon teas, were primarily for women, whereas company dinners were co-ed. Lunch, which was referred to as dinner in pastimes, was not as heavy a meal, nor as ornate, as supper, the last meal of the day. Plates and portions were dainty and modest, though not necessarily in decoration. The following luncheon set was described by C. E. Brady in "Suggestions for Table Service," which appeared in the May 1890 edition of *The Art Amateur.* While the artwork was praised as being commensurate with the European pieces that were used in conjunction, the artist's talent for china painting was unfairly downplayed, reasoned as the result of an able teacher and her own good taste:

> *"Not long ago one of our young matrons gave an elaborate luncheon, at which, with a complete change of plates for each, six courses out of ten were served with china of her own decorating, which was in nowise put in the shade by the Crown Derby and Dresden that alternated with it. . . And this lady has had no exceptional advantages, merely good instruction, such as is to be had here at home, supplemented by energy and taste. She left a goodly array of charmingly decorated pieces in her mother's sideboard, and is now filling her own.*
> *"In this case, that portion of the service which was home decoration included wild flowers, fish, birds, views and orchids. . ."*

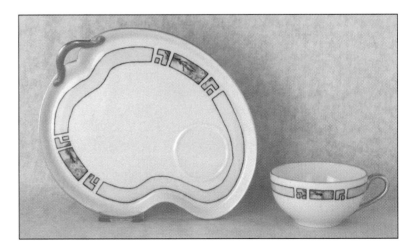

Two-piece sandwich set; single-handled plate; 7⅛"w; Flowering rose branch, bands and ground color executed in overglaze paints; burnished gold rim and handles; Signed: "McD"; Blank: Japan; ca. 1925-1935; $25-35.

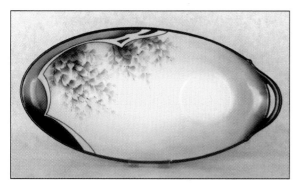

Sandwich set; single-handled plate, 10½"w (missing cup); Maidenhair ferns and ground color executed in overglaze paints; Blank: T & V rectangle, Limoges, France; ca. 1892-1907; $20-30.

Three-piece luncheon set; plate, 7½"dia; Conventional floral border design executed in overglaze paints; white enamel flower centers; burnished gold rims and handle; Blank: Germany; ca. 1914-1918; $30-40.

In a 1929 catalog from china supplier W. A. Maurer, these same pieces are pictured as part of a tea set, as well as sold individually. It appears that china painters may have bought sets to save money, but split them up to create their own assemblages that satisfied theirs, or their customer's, needs. Oftentimes china painters assembled their own sets from porcelains manufactured by various factories, noticeable by the different backstamps on pieces that comprise a set. Additionally, economical practices may have been employed, and pieces of decorated china may have served more than one purpose.

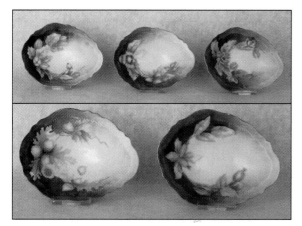

Set of five individual nut dishes; 5"w; Various nuts and ground colors executed in overglaze paints; burnished gold rims; Signed: "L. V."; Blank: Royal wreath, O. & E. G.; 1898-1918; $50-75.

Set of four individual nut bowls; 3½"dia (unfinished decoration); Conventional-style acorn and oak design executed in overglaze paints; mother-of-pearl luster interiors; Blank: crowned double-headed bird, MZ, Austria; ca. 1884-1909; $40-50.

Individual bonbon dish; 3½"dia; Conventional-style butterflies executed in overglaze paints; burnished gold border bands and feet; Signed: "From Beatrice, Xmas '07"; Blank: Royal wreath, O. & E.G., Austria; $25-35.

Lobster or shrimp salad bowl; 10½"w by 7¾"d; Seashells, seaweeds, and exterior ground colors executed in overglaze paints; white enamel embellishments; burnished gold rim; Blank: H and Co., Limoges, France; ca. 1888-1896; $75-125.

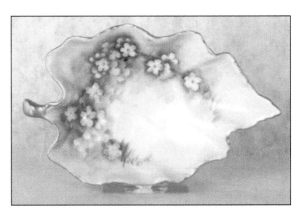

Individual bonbon dish; 4⅝"w by 2¾"d; Forget-me-nots and ground color executed in overglaze paints; burnished gold; Blank: T & V rectangle, Limoges, France; 1892-1907; $15-25.

Pickle dish; 11¼"w; Maidenhair ferns and ground color executed in overglaze paints; burnished gold border and rim; Signed: "Ida Lyston Paine"; Blank: T & V rectangle, Limoges, France; ca. 1892-1907; $35-55.

Sherbet; 3⅛"h; Daisies and ground color executed in overglaze paints; mother-of-pearl luster interior; burnished gold border, rim, and foot; Signed: "M. Paddock"; Blank: Epiag, Czechoslovakia; ca. 1920-1939; $25-35.

Sherbet (3"h) and plate (6"dia); Poppies and ground colors executed in overglaze paints; burnished gold rims and foot rim; Signed: "S. M. E."; Blank: sherbet, Thomas shield, Bavaria; plate, J & C, Bavaria; ca. 1908-1918; $30-40.

Sherbet or punch cup? The same cup could be used to serve either, and the blank was listed under a variety of headings in china catalogs. The daisy-decorated cup shown above was once part of a sandwich set. Since punch was not a drink that was served with lunch, in all likelihood this cup was used for dessert.

Although no catalog depicts a plate for use with a sherbet cup, the artist of the poppy-decorated set must have decided to combine the two as a set. (Note the two different porcelain manufacturers.)

The place setting, or cover, was basically the same as for a formal dinner. (Refer to Chapter Four for more detail.) Nut cups were located to the above right of the individual service plate. Pickles, olives, celery, bonbons, nut dishes, and cracker jars were placed on the table when the meal began. The centerpiece was a jardiniere, loving cup, or vase containing ferns or flowers.

Typical menus began with hors d'oerves, such as oysters, canapés, or grapefruit in winter, strawberries in summer. Soup followed this course, which was served in two-handled cups. Entrées such as chops or fish replaced the roast, accompanied by potatoes and vegetables. The meal was completed by a frozen dessert and fancy cakes, then crackers, cheese, and coffee. Later on, tea and chocolate were offered as beverages, in addition to, or replacing, coffee.

Honey dish; 7⅛"dia; Clover, wheat, ground color, and feet executed in overglaze paints; white enamel embellishments; burnished gold rim; Blank: Bavaria; ca. 1891-1914; $25-45.

Also listed as a bonbon and olive dish in china catalogs.

A Clover Luncheon

"The place cards were white, with a four-leaved clover pasted on each. The first course was fruit, then fish creamed in ramekins, Saratoga chips, pear salad, cheese wafers, olives, nuts, cheese balls with bar-le-duc. A sherbet, small cakes and iced grape juice completed the repast. After luncheon a long walk was taken through the fields to hunt four-leafed clovers. On return tiny hot biscuits with clover honey were served on the porch, with tea."

"Dame Curtsey's" Book of Party Pastimes for the Up-to-Date Hostess, Ellye Howell Glover, 1912 (2nd edition)

Tutti Frutti

In 1884, Mrs. D. A. Lincoln, principal of the Boston Cooking School from its incorporation in 1879 until 1885, wrote in the *Boston Cooking School Cook Book* that ripe fruit was particularly appropriate at the breakfast table. Fruit could be substituted for soup at lunch, or offered at the end of a meal.

There was a great variety of specialized porcelain pieces designed to hold specific fruits. Porcelain whiteware, as shown in china catalogs, depict various 9-inch diameter round or square serving bowls offered with smaller round dishes for individual use. When not in use, these, too, were kept on the sideboard.

Berry set; bowl, 8⅛"dia; individual saucers, 5⅛"dia; *Various fruits and ground colors executed in overglaze paints; burnished gold rims; Bowl: shield, C. & E. Carstens, Germany, ca. 1904–1933; individual saucers: wreath and star, R. S. Germany; 1904–1938; $200–275.*

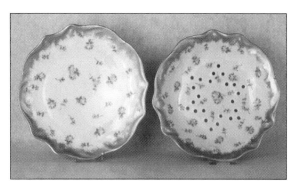

Berry bowl and plate; *Roses and forget-me-nots executed in overglaze paints; burnished gold borders and rims; Stamped: "William Lycett"; Atlanta; ca. 1920–1938; $50–75.*

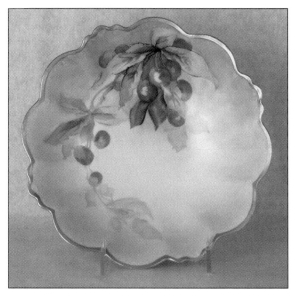

Fruit bowl; 9¼"dia; *Cherries and ground colors executed in overglaze paints; burnished gold rim; Blank: crowned double-headed bird, MZ, Austria; ca. 1884–1909; $65–85.*

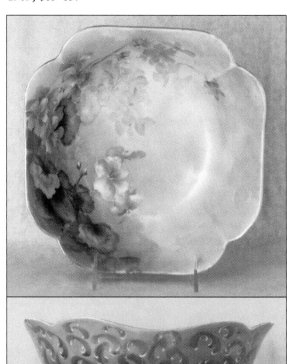

Fruit bowl; 8¾"sq; *Geraniums, ground colors, and scroll pattern executed in overglaze paints; burnished gold rim; Blank: none; ca. 1880–1900; $60–80.*

Footed fruit bowl; 7½"dia by 3½"h; Conventional-style floral design and ground color exectued in over-glaze paints; mother-of-pearl luster interior ground panels; burnished gold rim and feet; Blank: none; ca. 1910–1935; $40–60.

Berry bowl and plate; bowl, 3¾"h; plate, 7¾"dia; Currants and ground colors executed in overglaze paints; burnished gold borders, rims, and feet; Signed: "L. B. S."; Blank: T & V rectangle, Limoges, France; ca. 1892–1907; $100–135.

Pierced berry bowls that allowed for drainage, with plates to catch the drips, were also listed as nut bowls and ice bowls in china catalogs. In this example the fruit decoration provides the clue to its intended use. Nut bowls were decorated with earth-toned designs. According to studies published in period art magazines, ice bowls were decorated with conventional designs.

Three piece berry set; handled tray; 10⅞"w by 9¼"d; Blackberries and ground colors executed in overglaze paints; burnished gold scrolls and rims; Signed: "Slocum"; Blank: Giraud, Limoges, France; ca. 1920s; $100–150.

Berries were commonly served with cream and powdered sugar.

Gooseberries are a common motif on pieces of American painted porcelain. They remain popular in Europe, particularly in Great Britain, where they have been grown in gardens since the reign of Henry VIII. Gooseberries were brought to America by colonists in the seventeenth century.

In North America, they are grown on a small scale today, but shoppers are more likely to find them canned rather than fresh. Pale green is the color of the most common kind of gooseberry, but there also are red and yellow ones.

Currants belong to the gooseberry family, and are available in red, black, and white (which are actually transparent). They grow wild on the West Coast, but only have limited cultivation today. They, too, can be found depicted on various porcelain forms.

Wild strawberries had been consumed for thousands of years. They were so plentiful in North America that few people bothered to cultivate them until early in the nineteenth century. These new berries, which were a cross between Virginia scarlets and a Chilean species, were twice the size of those found in native woodlands. Strawberries became an extravagance, especially when served with rich cream.

The growth of the railroad industry fueled the expansion of strawberry cultivation by mid-century. By the 1880s, more than 100,000 acres in Florida, Tennessee, Arkansas, and Louisiana were dedicated to their farming, shipped to markets all over the country by refrigerated railroad cars.

Double handled spoon tray; 9¼"w by 4"d; Burnished gold rim and handles; Blank: none; ca. 1920-1930; $20-30.

Double handled spoon tray; 6"w by 2⅞"d; Burnished gold; Blank: wreath and star, R. S. Germany; ca. 1904-1938; $15-25.

"Berries, of course, are to be eaten with a spoon," proclaimed Hugo Ziemann and Mrs. F. L. Gillette in *The White House Cook Book*, which was originally published in 1887. To complete the porcelain outfit, there also were berry spoon holders that held the specialized utensils and coordinated with these decorations.

Berry spoon holder; 9¾"w; Strawberries and ground colors executed in overglaze paints; burnished gold rim and handles; Signed: "A. E. Pierce" (attributed to Anna E. Pierce, Milwaukee, ca. 1910-1918); Blank: crossed lines, KPM; ca. 1904-1927; $20-30.

Berry spoon holder; 10"w; Blackberries and ground colors executed in overglaze paints; burnished gold rim and handles; Blank: Bavaria; ca. 1891-1914; $25-45.

This same china blank also was listed as an olive dish in catalogs. The decoration provides the clue. Here, the berry designs indicate that these pieces would have held berry spoons.

Three-piece tea set; teapot holds 28 oz.; Roses, border bands, and ground colors executed in overglaze paints; white enamel embellishments; burnished gold rims, handles, scrolls, feet, and knobs; Blank: Favorite, Bavaria; ca.1908-1918; $175-250.

Tea set or coffee set? Although the spout on this pot is placed low like a coffee pot, and its shape taller and more ovoid than a teapot, several china catalogs listed this set as a tea set. It was for serving iced tea, rather than hot tea.

"Iced tea (Russian) is served a great deal with dinner during the summer months."

Imperial Cook Book, *1894, rev. ed., Mrs. Grace Townsend*

To Serve or Not to Serve: Claret and Grape Juice

"Water bottles are now very common, and may be arranged here and there accompanied by a bowl of ice," wrote Mrs. Grace Townsend in *Imperial Cook Book* (1894). Water, and sometimes grape juice as well as lemonade, were served from pitchers that varied in shape and height. These liquids were poured into tumblers which had been painted to match.

Tumbler; 3⅜"h; Roses and ground colors executed in overglaze paints; burnished gold rim; Signed: (illegible); Blank: La Seynie, PP, Limoges, France; ca. 1903–1917; $18–25.

Claret pitcher; 9¾"h; Conventional-style floral design and ground color executed in overglaze paints, with burnished gold outlines; burnished gold handle edges; Signed: "V. B. Chase"; Blank: none; ca. 1890–1914; $40–60.

Those who served wine at a luncheon could offer a decanter of claret and one of sherry. Claret was served from a tall, tapered pitcher with a small opening. Its shape helped keep the liquid cool while allowing the wine to breathe. This same pitcher also was listed in some china catalogs as a grape juice jug. Its use can be determined by the time period of the decoration. Specifically, whether it dated before Prohibition, when the Eighteenth Amendment went into effect in 1920, or after. (It must be noted that some states were dry as early as 1916.)

The Setting

Breakfast could be taken from a tray while still in bed, but usually was eaten in the morning room or in the dining room, or sometimes even the parlor. On the other hand, lunch was served only in the dining room.

By the 1920s, the breakfast room or breakfast nook supplanted the dining room for the first meal of the day. This alcove or room was part of, or adjacent to, the kitchen, and it was cozier and more convenient. No longer was a large table needed to accommodate families, for as time passed, families decreased in size. Eventually lunch also was eaten here, and family dinners as well. The dining room today, while still containing the most expensive furniture and continuing the tradition of displaying a family's treasured china, is appreciated more for appearances than actual use.

Card Parties

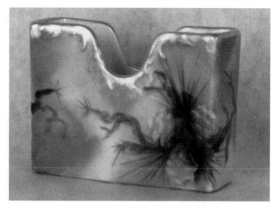

The usual hour at which leave was taken after a luncheon was three o'clock, unless there was to be entertainment, such as a card party. Games of bridge sometimes followed luncheon, lasting until six-thirty. This party was followed by tea. (Evening card parties involved both women and men, and began after dinner at nine o'clock.)

In the latter part of the nineteenth century, any form of gambling, including card playing, was frowned upon as immoral. As the first decade of the twentieth century passed, card playing became permissible for women as well as men. Although card games became agreeable recreation, playing for money was strictly forbidden, unless the occasion was a fundraiser for charity.

Card holder; 3¾"w by 1⁵⁄₁₆"d by 2¾"h; Pine cones and ground colors executed in overglaze paints; burnished gold border and rim; Signed: "S. A. P."; Blank: Favorite, Bavaria; ca. 1908-1918; $18-28.

Etiquette advisers warned of the pitfalls of gambling. Helen L. Roberts was one such adviser who wrote in *Putnam's Handbook of Etiquette:*

"Games that are played for cash rewards give rise to situations in society that are frequently most embarrassing. Many a man or woman in moderate circumstances is seriously annoyed, or even temporarily straitened in funds, on being caught in circumstances whence it is impossible to escape until more than one ill-spared dollar has been lost."

Double-handled sandwich tray, 14½"w; Various nuts and ground colors executed in overglaze paints: Burnished gold rim and handles. Signed: "WANDS" (William D. Wands, Chicago, 1910-1916); Blank: crown, crossed scepters, Rosenthal, Bavaria; $55-65.

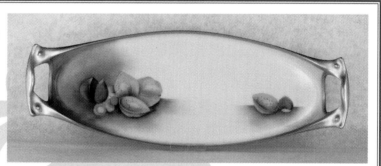

A Novel Nut Card Party

"A hostess wishing to add a touch of novelty to her afternoon card party . . . did so in this manner . . . For refreshments, nut sandwiches, with chicken salad, olives, and cheese nuts were served with nut ice cream and nut cake. Glacéd nuts were the sweet, and salted nuts were passed."

"Dame Curtsey's" Book of Party Pastimes for the Up-to-Date Hostess by Ellye Howell Glover, 1912 (2nd ed.)

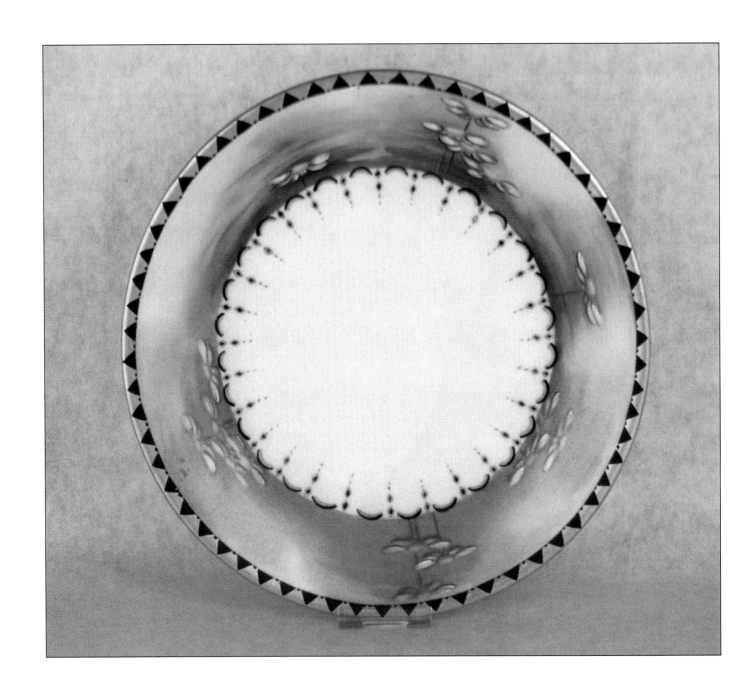

"SERVING DINNER IS A CEREMONY IN WHICH THE HOUSEWIFE
TAKES SPECIAL PRIDE. WHAT AN IMPORTANT PART FINE CHINA
PLAYS IN MAKING THE DINNER A DELIGHTFUL EVENT. THE
DINING TABLE IS THE SCENE OF FAMILY LIFE, AND
ENTERTAINMENT."

Thayer & Chandler China Catalog
September 1923

Chapter Seven

The Dinner Party

Dinner became the main meal when men began working in places too far away to return home for a midday repast. By the late nineteenth century, dinner was the one meal where the entire family—including the father, mother, five to ten children, and perhaps a set of grandparents or maiden aunts—would gather together. Even everyday family dinners consisted of multiple courses. Food, drink, and of course, manners, were of central importance to luxurious living, echoed by the choice of location for the meal, which was the dining room. (Servants ate and prepared food in the kitchen.)

Since abundant food was equated with wealth and hospitality, giving a company dinner was a momentous affair. "An invitation to a dinner is the highest social compliment that can be offered," wrote Maud C. Cooke in *Our Deportment*. Handwritten or engraved invitations on heavy cream-colored paper were sent out ten days to two weeks in advance. "It is hardly necessary to say that only serious illness or the most urgent business is ever allowed to nullify at the eleventh hour an invitation to dinner which one has formally accepted," wrote Helen L. Roberts in *Putnam's Handbook of Etiquette*. "To urge a frivolous excuse, or mere change of one's mind, as a reason for not putting in an appearance at a lady's dinner table, on the evening and hour appointed, is the most serious social offense that a man or woman can possibly commit." Once accepted, breaking an engagement could result in social strangulation.

Party Time

Guests arriving for a dinner party gathered in the host and hostess's parlor. After everyone had arrived, the host led the way to the dining room. "Each gentleman should be given a card on entering the dressing room, with the name of the lady whom he is to escort to the dining room, and the letters R or L, also on the card, indicating to the right or left of the hostess," wrote Maria Willett Howard in *Lowney's Cook Book*. Each man offered the lady assigned to him his right arm. He proceeded to escort her to her seat to the left of his, indicated by a place card on top of the folded napkin, or above the service plate. When gloves were worn in the nineteenth century, they were drawn off and laid upon one's lap under the napkin once a person was seated. Ladies also drew in their voluminous skirts in order to avoid crowding their neighbors.

> *"It is in better taste to take a little of every dish than to imply, by our picking and choosing, a too abundant provision on the part of our hostess, or that she has been unsuccessful in pleasing our fancy."*
>
> "THE TOUCHSTONE OF GOOD MANNERS"
> MRS. BURTON KINGSLAND
> *The Ladies' Home Journal*
> JANUARY 1896

Dinner was quietly announced when the soup tureen (with the soup at the boiling point) and the soup cups were in place before the hostess's seat if she was going to do the serving. The soup, salad, and dessert were the only courses to be served by the hostess. Carving the meat was the responsibility of the host. As a rule, the lady to the right of the host, or the eldest lady, was served first.

According to *Buckeye Cookery and Practical Housekeeping*, "A sensible bill of fare is soup, fish with one vegetable, a roast with one or two vegetables and a salad and cheese, and a dessert." Dinners in *The White House Cook Book* also began with soup, but were followed by one entrée, three vegetables, and a side dish. Two kinds of desserts were included, and the meal finished off with coffee accompanied by cheese or fruit. Fannie Merritt Farmer included eighteen different dinner menus in *The Boston Cooking-School Cook Book*. Her sample menus began with a first course of soup and a second course of fish, fowl, or meat, with accompanying vegetables. A vegetable salad with dressing might be offered after this, followed by dessert, such as puddings and pies, then fruit, and coffee. Sometimes two choices were offered for each course, such as two kinds of soup (one clear and one cream), or two kinds of game (pheasant and duck). This kind of generosity could easily double the required number of porcelain dishes as well.

> ## *"Each course may be served on dishes different from the other courses ..."*
>
> Our Deportment, or Manners and Customs of Polite Society
> MAUD C. COOKE, 1902

Farmer, like many other cookbook authors, also presented menus for full course dinners, which to her meant a twelve-course meal—double the number of courses for a family dinner. Typically, though, the number of courses served at a formal dinner was more variable. According to *Lowney's Cook Book*, a company dinner could vary from eight to twelve courses, with ten being average. Its author's advice was to "Avoid repetition; if oysters appear in the first course, they must not appear again." Likewise, Isabella Beeton advised "that two brown or white sauces . . . not follow each other; and that each dish should vary in color and taste from that served before and after it."

In the Beginning

If twelve courses were served, dinner began with hors d'oeurves. Little Neck Clams, canapés, oysters, or fruit cocktail could be offered. Whatever was chosen, it was generally in place when the company assembled.

Two-piece, double-handled bouillon cup and saucer; Conventional style design executed in burnished gold and outlined with overglaze paint; burnished gold rims and handles; Blank: T & V rectangle, Limoges, France; ca. 1892-1907; $25-35.

Two-piece double-handled bouillon cup and saucer; Roses and border bands executed in overglaze paints; burnished gold scrolls, border bands, rims, and handles; Blank: T & V rectangle, Limoges, France; ca. 1892-1907; $35-45.

Set of two, two-piece, double-handled bouillon cups and saucers; Burnished gold rims, feet, cup interiors, handles, and monogram; Blank: crown, crossed scepters, Rosenthal, Selb, Bavaria; ca. 1908-1933; $50-80.

Set of two, three-piece, double-handled and covered bouillon cups and saucers; Burnished gold borders, rims, handles, and feet; Blank: cups, T & V rectangle; saucers, star; both marked Limoges, France; ca. 1891-1914; $65-90.

Double-handled cream soup cup; 4½"dia (missing plate); Roses and ground color executed in overglaze paints; mother-of-pearl luster interior; burnished gold rim and handles; Blank: Bavaria; ca. 1891-1914; $15-25.

Also listed as a bonbon bowl in some china catalogs.

Cracker jar; 9"dia; Wild roses and ground colors executed in overglaze paints; burnished gold handles; Signed: "A.S.S."; Blank: Royal wreath, O. & E. G.; 1898-1918; $50-75.

Crackers were kept in, and served from, biscuit or cracker jars, although trays could be employed. When not in use cracker jars were stored on the sideboard.

The second course was the soup course. Clear soups were served in double-handled bouillon cups, 3½ inches in diameter and 2¼ inches high. This kind of soup was accompanied by bread sticks, small rolls, crackers, or croutons. Sometimes the cups had lids to help the soup stay hot.

Pair of soup plates; 9"dia; Sea shells, sea weeds and ground colors executed in overglaze paints; burnished gold rims; Signed: "ALB"; Blank: H & Co., Haviland, Limoges, France, 1876-1879; $30-50.

Soup plates such as these were never used for company dinners, for every period etiquette and cookbook states that soup was served in double-handled cups or bowls. These pieces probably were used for family meals instead.

Cream soups were served in shallower and wider cups that varied from 4½ to 5 inches in diameter, and about two inches high. These cups were double-handled as well. Cream soups were accompanied by croutons.

Contained Within

Commercially canned products were a novelty and expense when they were introduced. Serving guests sardines, for example, was quite an honor. However, the gaudy labels on these canned goods offended the Victorians' sense of good taste when it came to table decoration. Special porcelain containers were designed to hide the cans.

Canned goods first appeared on store shelves in 1880. The process originally was developed in response to the food shortages caused in France by British blockades during the Napoleonic Wars (1792-1813). In 1795, François Appert designed a preserving jar for foods. It was the British iron works of Donkin, Hall and Gamble that took this concept and adapted it, manufacturing tinned iron containers beginning in 1812. Eleven years later in 1823, Thomas Kensett of New York first patented the tin can. Tin cans originally were handmade, followed in 1847 by machine-stamped cans. It wasn't until 1865 that thinner cans which could be used with can openers were available.

Sardine box; 5¼"w by 4-3/16"d by 1⅝"h; (missing serving platter); Fish and sea weeds executed in overglaze paints; white enamel highlights; burnished gold rim and scrolls; Blank: T & V rectangle, Limoges, France; ca. 1892-1907; $50-75.

Small fish were the favored ornament of sardine boxes.

Sardines were one of the first canned foods, initially processed in 1819. They were suggested as a side dish during the soup course. An article in the November 1900 issue of *The Art Interchange* also mentioned that a sardine box and tray for lemons was a "useful addition" to the lunch table. Covered porcelain boxes were manufactured and decorated, often with fish, to conceal the can's label while giving diners knowledge as to content.

With the invention and development of electric refrigerators in 1913, which became widely available by the late 1920s, canned foods were less of a necessity, and by that time, no longer a new product. The convenience of canned goods, however, assured their place in meal preparation, as well as on tables.

Served with Relish

"Salted almonds, olives, celery, and radishes may be served in dainty small dishes placed when the table is set for dinner; almonds and olives may remain throughout the meal," advised Mrs. Rorer in the June 1898 issue of *The Ladies' Home Journal*. Celery, radishes, or olives usually were passed after the soup, and salted almonds could be passed between any of the courses. They were classified among the few acceptable "finger foods." (In the Victorian era, it was considered uncouth to touch most foods with one's fingers.) Leafy celery tops were removed and the stalks broken into edible portions which were dipped into salt. Radishes also were salted.

"…fancy dishes, unlike any of the rest, may be used to pass relishes, such as olives, and add greatly to the beauty of the table serve."

Our *Deportment, or the Manners and Customs of Polite Society*
MAUD C. COOKE, 1902

By 1912, dining habits had changed somewhat. Maria Willet Howard declared in *Lowney's Cook Book* that celery was to be passed with oysters, radishes or olives with the fish course. No matter when they were served, these side dishes remained choice offerings for formal meals.

Double-handled relish dish; 5½"w by 3¼"d; Burnished gold border, rims, and handles; Blank: shield, Prov. Sxe. E. S., Germany; ca. 1902-1938; $15-25.

Relish dish; 9"w by 3¾"d; Clematis and ground colors executed in overglaze paints; burnished gold rim and handles; Signed: "M. GATE(S?)"; Blank: crown, crossed scepters, Rosenthal; ca. 1891-1907; $30-40.

Double-handled relish dish; 9¼"w by 4"d; Burnished gold borders, rims, and handles; Blank: none; ca. 1920-1930; $25-45.

Double-handled pickle or olive dish; 9½"w by 5⅞"d; Conventional-style acanthus leaf border design executed in overglaze paints; burnished gold border, rim, and handles; Signed: "J. Pugh"; Blank: GDA, France; ca. 1900-1941; $30-40.

Double-handled olive or radish dish; 6⅞"d; Daisies executed in overglaze paints, burnished gold rim and handle; Signed: "S. M. Plachter"; Blank: GDA, Limoges, France; ca. 1900-1925; $35-45.

Also listed as bonbon dish in china catalogs.

Double-handled olive or radish dish; 7"dia; Conventional-style fruits executed in overglaze paints; burnished gold rim, banding, and handles; Signed: "R. C. Briccs"; Blank: crown, crossed scepters, Rosenthal Donatello, Selb, Bavaria; ca. 1908-1933; $35-45.

Also listed as bonbon dish in china catalogs.

Double-handled olive or radish dish; 7"dia; Conventional-style nasturtiums and border color executed in overglaze paints; yellow enamel flower centers; burnished gold handles; Signed: "MEYER"; Blank: Hutschenreuther, Selb, Bavaria; 1856-1920; $35-45.

Also listed as bonbon dish in china catalogs.

Ring-handled olive dish; 6⅞"dia; Daisies, border band, and ground color executed in overglaze paints; burnished gold rim and handle; Signed: "J. Hanke"; Blank: Royal Epiag, 1920-1945; $35-45.

Also listed as a butterball tray and bonbon dish in china catalogs.

Ring-handled olive; 7⅜"dia; Heliotrope executed in overglaze paints; etched and burnished gold border; burnished gold handle; Blank: T & V rectangle, Limoges, France; ca. 1892-1907; $35-45.

Also listed as a butterball tray and bonbon dish in china catalogs.

Olive dish; 6¼"w by 4¾"d; Roses and ground color executed in overglaze paints; burnished gold rim; Signed: "R. S. (B.?) from S. D. C., Christmas, 1904"; Blank: T & V rectangle, Deposse, Limoges, France; $18-30.

At one time growing celery was labor intensive. Celery had to be blanched by surrounding it with piles of soil that preserved its color and sweetness. As the plant was improved during the eighteenth century, its use became more common among the wealthy who could afford expensive produce.

From the 1860s through the 1880s, celery was given a prominent position on the dining table. It was served in its own stand or vase made from decorated glass or silver, both of which were luxury materials.

In the 1880s, a new self-blanching commercial variety of celery that was easier to grow was developed. As its availability increased it became a more ordinary vegetable, and its display on the tabletop changed from a vertical position to a horizontal one. Such a change relegated celery to a less prominent place, reflecting its change in status. Low celery dishes replaced the stands as serving pieces.

Celery dish; 12"w by 5¼"d; Roses, forget-me-nots, and ground colors executed in overglaze paints; enamel embellishments; burnished gold rim; Signed: "McKee"; Blank: Royal wreath, O. & E.G., Austria; 1899-1918; $35-55.

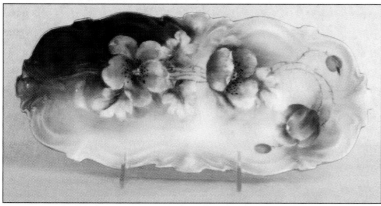

Celery dish; 12"w by 5"d; Poppies and ground colors executed in overglaze paints; burnished gold rim; Signed: "E. ZOOST"; Blank: none; ca. 1900-1920; $35-55.

Double-handled celery dish; 9⅞"w by 4⅝"d; Violets and ground colors executed in overglaze paints; burnished gold rim, handles, and scrolls; Signed: "Luken" (Minnie A. Luken, Luken Art Studios, Chicago, 1895-1926); Blank: Bavaria; $20-35.

Handled celery dish; 10¾"w by 7"d; Roses executed in overglaze paints; burnished gold rim and handle; Signed: "Maude Kendall"; Blank: none; ca. 1900-1920; $50-75.

Also listed as a sandwich tray in china catalogs.

Celery sets in china catalogs consisted of a celery boat or long dish with twelve celery dips for salt. Maria Parloa wrote in her column "Everything About the House" in the November 1891 issue of *The Ladies' Home Journal* that celery was served in long flat dishes. She recommended that it be put on the table with meat and other vegetables, but removed before dessert was placed on the table. But as new, heartier strains were developed, celery lost its cachet. By 1900, celery no longer held its special status, although it continued to be offered with dinner.

Pressed for Service

Footed bowl; 5½"dia; Conventional-style floral executed in overglaze paints and enamels; burnished gold flower centers, bands, rim, and feet; Blank: Bavaria; ca. 1891-1914; $20-40.

Russian compote; 8½"w; Conventional-style grape border and ground color executed in overglaze paints; burnished gold outlines, border, and rim; Signed: "McCarthy, Schulz, Stuhl"; Blank: UNO-IT, Favorite, Bavaria; ca. 1908-1918; $35-50.

Single handled comport; 10¾"w; Wild roses and ground colors executed in overglaze paints; burnished gold border, rim, and handle; Signed: "Milne"; Blank: Limoges scroll, W. G. & Co., Limoges, France; ca. 1901; $45-65.

Also listed as a sandwich tray in china catalogs.

Bowl; 9¼"dia; Burnished gold border, inner band, and rim; Blank: none; ca. 1920-1930; $25-45.

Covered dish; 8¾"dia; Roses and ground color executed in overglaze paints; burnished gold handles and rim; Blank: horse and archer, Peerless, Bavaria; ca. 1935-1955; $50-75.

Open casserole; 8¼"dia; Roses and border band executed in overglaze paints; mother-of-pearl luster interior; platinum rim and panel outlines; Stamped: "Royal-Rochester Studios"; Blank: none; ca. 1918-1930; $35-45.

Matches ramekin pictured on page 143.

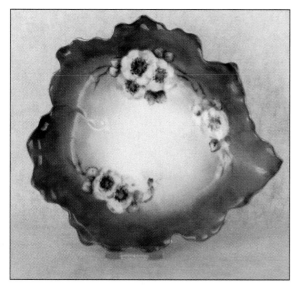

Leaf-shaped dish; 6⅞"w by 6⅛"d; Primrose and ground color executed in overglaze paints; burnished gold rim; Blank: wavy line, Z. S. & Co., Bavaria; ca. 1880; $30-45.

Single handled dish; 6¼"w; Cherries and rim color executed in overglaze paints; Signed: "F. M."; Blank: M.Z., Altrohlau, Austria; ca. 1910-1919; $20-30.

Pile on the Protein

The third course consisted of bouchées, rissoles, croquettes, or sweetbreads. These were small pastry shells filled with creamed meat and served on plates.

The fourth course was baked, boiled, or fried fish, accompanied by cole slaw, dressed cucumbers, tomatoes, or potatoes if fried fish were offered. The whole fish was placed on a long, narrow fish platter, with individual servings placed onto fish plates. Bone dishes, which were crescent-shaped, were located directly above the place plate. Sauce boats also were requisite.

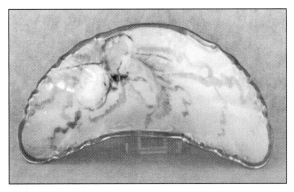

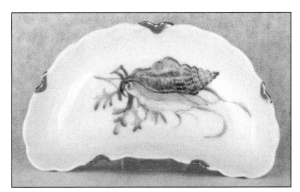

Bone dish; 6⅝"w; Seashells and seaweeds executed in overglaze paints; burnished gold border and rim; Taped to bottom, "hand painted by Mildred Steeberg"; Blank: none; ca. 1890-1915; $15-25.

Bone dish; 6"w; Seashells and seaweeds executed in overglaze paints; burnished gold trim; Signed: (illegible); Blank: H & Co., Haviland, France; 1888-1896; $15-25.

Sauce boat and plate; 6"w; Burnished gold borders, rims, base rim, and handle; Blank: Germany; ca. 1920-1930; $25-45.

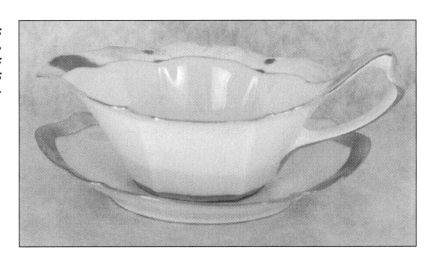

Gravy boat with attached stand; 9½"w; Roses and ground colors executed in overglaze paints; burnished gold rims; Blank: T & V rectangle, Limoges, France; ca. 1892-1917; $55-75. Matches covered sugar bowl pictured on page 91.

Gravy boat with attached stand; 8¾"w; Roses and border bands executed in overglaze paints; burnished gold borders, rims, and monogram; Signed: "R.G."; Blank: Haviland, France; ca. 1894-1931; $55-65.

The design of double-lipped gravy boats was based upon eighteenth century silver models of continental Europe.

Jelly tray; 7"dia; Conventional-style flowers executed in overglaze paints; mother-of-pearl luster bands; burnished gold urns, rim, and handles; Signed: "Phoebe Pelton"; Blank: none; ca. 1900-1920; $25-35.

Also listed as a radish dish in china catalogs.

Meat platter; 17⅝"w by 11½"d; Carnations and ground color executed in overglaze paints; white enamel embellishments; burnished gold rim; Blank: H & Co., Limoges, France; ca. 1891; $225-275.

The fifth course consisted of venison or mutton, spring lamb, or fillet of beef, offered with gravy and side dishes of potatoes, jelly, and a choice of vegetable. Jelly was served in open dishes. "Jellies and sauces, when not to be eaten as a dessert, should be helped on the dinner-plate, not on a small side dish as was the former usage," wrote Hugo Ziemann and Mrs. F. L. Gillette in *The White House Cook Book*.

The sixth course, known as the entrée, was a light meat or fish. Sometimes the entrée was served in a ramekin. As late as 1942, the following advice was presented in *America's Cook Book*: ". . . the service will be expedited if portions are prepared in individual ramekins or casseroles so that they may be brought, piping hot, from the kitchen." A gelatin or jelly frequently accompanied the entrée, presented in special molds.

After so many meat dishes, the seventh course consisted of a vegetable, such as mushrooms, cauliflower, asparagus, or artichokes. Punch would have constituted the eighth course. "Punch, when served, always precedes the game course," advised Fannie Merritt Farmer, author of *The Boston Cooking-School Cook Book* referring to Roman punch. Roman punch was really a sorbet, not a liquid drink. It served to cleanse one's palate. This refreshment would have constituted the eighth course.

To the Nines

For the ninth course, game was offered, along with a vegetable salad, a dish adopted from the French. Game was one of the most abundant foods available to early American settlers, and a prominent source of protein to the colonists. Later on game became an epicure's fancy.

Pair of game plates; left plate, 8¾"dia; right plate, 9⁷⁄₁₆"dia; Stylized pheasant, quail, and landscapes executed in overglaze paints; burnished gold rims; Signed: (illegible); Blank: Bavaria; ca. 1903-1917; $55-75.

*Salad bowl; 10"dia; Conventional-style **fleur-de-lis** design executed in overglaze paints and burnished gold; burnished gold rim and base border; Signed: "Louise M. Pflaum"; Blank: crown and scepter, Silesia; ca. 1906-1916; $60-80.*

Salad plate; 9½"w by 5¼"d; Sweet peas executed in overglaze paints; burnished gold rim; Blank: none; ca. 1900-1924; $35-50.

Also listed as a relish dish and cookie tray in china catalogs.

A Victorian vegetable salad might include lettuce, mustard greens and cress, chicory, radishes, cucumber, endive, red cabbage, beet root, celery, and after 1880, tomatoes. Prior to the 1870s, the commercial production of lettuce was limited. California lettuce was unavailable before 1900, and iceberg lettuce, which was developed to withstand long-distance shipping, wasn't created until 1903. "It is not so many years ago that salads were considered a luxury only to be found on the tables of the wealthy; to-day a wider knowledge of cookery has taught the house-wife who has to set a table with a small income that there is no more economical, wholesome dish than a well-made salad," wrote Isabel Gordon Curtis in 1909 in *Mrs. Curtis's Cook Book.*

Salad could be prepared beforehand on individual crescent-shaped or round plates and served to diners by a servant, or distributed at the table by the hostess who filled individual plates from a large salad bowl. As an alternative, salad could be offered after the main course, along with cheese.

Crescent-shaped plates were depicted in *The Art Amateur* throughout the 1880s and 1890s. These were placed above the dinner plate. Its crescent shape was well-suited to accommodating the round shape of the center plate. Circular salad plates were placed to the left or the right of the dinner plate, depending on the cookbook authority.

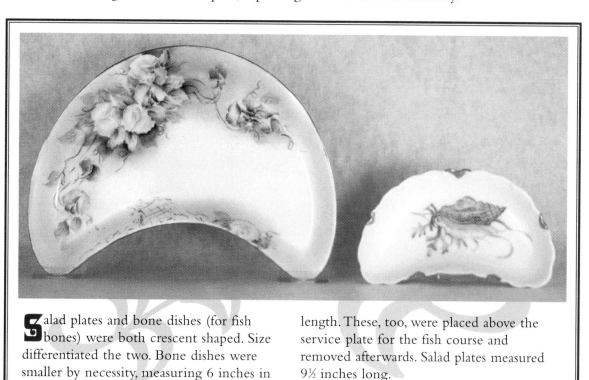

Salad plates and bone dishes (for fish bones) were both crescent shaped. Size differentiated the two. Bone dishes were smaller by necessity, measuring 6 inches in length. These, too, were placed above the service plate for the fish course and removed afterwards. Salad plates measured 9½ inches long.

Ramekins: Dating by Shape and by Decoration

Rich soufflés and custards were favored sweets meant to impress guests, but even family dinners could include these. One sample dinner menu given by Fannie Merritt Farmer in her book *The Boston Cooking-School Cook Book,* suggested Irish stew with dumplings as a first course; fish croquettes, dinner rolls, and radishes as a second course; custard soufflé and creamy sauce as a third course; finished up with crackers and cheese.

Soufflé literally means "puffed up." It is a delicate baked custard which may contain fruit, cheese, flaked fish, minced poultry, meat, or vegetables. Small portions proved quite adequate, especially after so many courses. Known as savories, these liquid desserts were served in delicate cups called ramekins (sometimes spelled "ramikins"), with a plate to match. Puff pastries with various fillings, such as cheese soufflé or marmalades and jellies, as well as puddings, were also baked and served in these.

Porcelain had the advantage of doubling as a baking dish. Soufflés could be prepared and baked in the individual ramekin dishes, for overglaze decoration, including the application of metals, required a temperature of over 1,350 degrees Fahrenheit to mature and fuse with the glaze. A 400 degree oven would not harm nor leach the decoration.

Ramekin; 4⅜"dia by 1½"h, and plate, 5³⁄₁₆"dia; Roses, forget-me-nots, and ground color executed in overglaze paints; burnished gold scrolls and rim; Signed: "Walters"; Blank: Bird, CT, ca. 1899-1918; $35-45.

Prior to 1899, ramekins were basically custard cups. An article titled "New Shapes in China" in the November 1899 edition of *The Art Interchange* includes a paragraph on ramekins: "A dainty ramekin is also a new addition to table ware. It varies from the old ones, by having a brim or shoulder, almost at right angles with the body. The small dish on which it stands has a similar edge."

By the 1920s, eating patterns had changed and other foods could be served in ramekins. A 1927 home economics book, *Everyday Foods* by Jessie W. Harris and Elisabeth V. Lacey, stated that, "Any scalloped, au gratin, or creamed vegetables may be cooked in individual porcelain baking dishes called ramekins. . . Mushrooms, cauliflower, eggplant, asparagus, baked beans, onions, and tomatoes make good ramekin dishes." But in cookbooks from the 1940s, these foods, as well as soufflés, were cooked and served from casseroles, not individual ramekins. Custards became the food commonly served in ramekins, now called custard cups in cookbooks. Like many other types of porcelain, ramekins were adapted to serve other foods, then passed into obsolescence as baked custards were replaced by varieties cooked on a stove top.

Ramekin; 4⅜"dia; Roses executed in overglaze paints; platinum rim; Stamped: "Royal Rochester" Studios; Blank: P. Co., Ohio; ca. 1918-1925; $10-15. Matches open casserole pictured on page 137.

This ramekin is of a more recent origin. Its collar is a simple ring. Its untinted ground reflects later fashion trends when the natural gloss from the glaze was considered an asset, rather than something to be toned down. Delicate yellow roses trim the collar, which is rimmed with platinum rather than the ubiquitous burnished gold prevalent in earlier American painted porcelains.

This porcelain piece was manufactured by the Ohio Pottery Company in Zanesville, Ohio. The backstamp dates between 1900 and 1923, but it is known that the company began producing hard paste porcelain dinnerware between 1918 and 1920. In 1923, the company, which also absorbed the American China Products Company of Chesterton, Indiana, became Fraunfelter China Company.

Both the Ohio Pottery Company and Fraunfelter China Company were one of the few American potteries that catered to the china painting market, producing porcelain equal in quality to European pieces, and at competitive prices.

The other "Royal Rochester" Studios mark on the bottom is a distributor's mark. Robeson Rochester Corporation, located in Rochester, New York, manufactured metallic products, including casserole holders, coffee urns, and baking pudding dishes. Fraunfelter China Company was one of the companies that made inserts for their tableware pieces. This ramekin probably fit into a silver metal holder, which would explain the use of platinum rather than gold on its rim. In all likelihood, it did not have a matching porcelain plate.

Just Desserts

The finale of formal dinners was a variety of desserts. Dessert dishes were arranged on the sideboard or on a separate side table. Tableware not needed for this course was removed, including the tablecloth. The tenth course was usually some sort of cold dessert, such as ices.

Set of six dessert plates; 6¾"dia; Various flowers and ground colors executed in overglaze paints; burnished gold rims; Signed: "P Putzki" (Paul Putzki, Washington, DC, ca. 1899-1915); Blank: crown, crossed scepters, Gotham, Austria; $75-110.

Dessert plate; 6⅜"dia; Garden landscape, garland border, and border band executed in overglaze paints; burnished gold border band and rim; Blank: none; ca. 1910-1920; $20-28.

Another dessert was offered for the eleventh course, such as ice cream and fancy cakes. Ice cream had always been a favored American treat. The founders of the United States are known to have indulged in eating it. George Washington, who owned the first ice cream freezer, spent two hundred dollars in one year to make this dessert! By 1790, ice cream was consumed by the wealthy as well as the common laborer. Its relative inexpensiveness was due to the availability of ice year round. Great blocks were cut from frozen ponds and lakes in the winter, insulated with straw and sawdust, and stored in ice houses or ice cellars.

Nancy Johnson invented the portable ice cream freezer in 1846, suitable for home use, but it was William G. Young who obtained a patent. Five years later, the production of ice cream burgeoned when Jacob Fussel, a Baltimore milk dealer, began manufacturing ice cream to use up excess cream, and discounted his product. He created what is believed to have been the first wholesale market for ice cream, eventually selling to other metropolitan markets, including Chicago, Cincinnati, Boston, New York, and St. Louis.

Home-made ice cream was packed in fancy round molds. Commercially-made ice cream was sold in bricks. Ice cream plates came in round, rectangular, and square shapes to accommodate the different types. Flat dessert plates sufficed for serving cake and pies as well. Bonbons also were passed after this course.

Ice cream bowl; 10⅝"w by 6¾"d by 2³⁄₁₆"h; Winter scene executed in overglaze paints; burnished gold border and rim; Signed: "F. L. Hey"; Blank: CFH/GDM; ca. 1920-1930; $100-125.

Cracker and cheese dish; 8½"dia; Conventional-style floral design executed in overglaze paints; mother-of-pearl luster ground; burnished gold ground, borders, and rims; Signed: (illegible); Blank: wreath and star, R. S. Tillowitz, Silesia; ca. 1920-1938; $85-125.

Two-piece cracker and cheese dish; 10"dia; Daisies and border bands executed in overglaze paints; mother-of-pearl luster ground; burnished gold rim; Signed: "M. G. '29"; Blank: circle, D & B, Japan; $85-125.

"Finger-bowls are brought on the table after the dessert is removed and before the fruit is served," wrote Cooke in *Our Deportment.* "They are usually placed before each individual on the fancy glass or china plate that is to be used for the fruit, a fancy doily being laid between the bowl and plate." Finger bowls were filled with warmed water, and had a rose geranium leaf or slice of lemon floating on top. Guests would dip their fingers one at a time in the water, rubbing the leaf or lemon between them to remove any food odor. Then they would dry their fingers on their napkin. "Remove bowl and doily at once to the right hand side, leaving plate free for the fruit."

Fruit, crackers, and cheese usually comprised the twelfth course, although sometimes it was included with *café noir* (black coffee). Crackers and cheese were served on special two-tiered dishes. The cheese was cut with a knife and a morsel was placed onto a piece of cracker or biscuit which had been broken into bite-sized pieces.

Cordial set; jug, 6½"h; cordial cups, 2¾"h; Currants executed in overglaze paints; mother-of-pearl luster stems; bright gold cup interiors; burnished gold neck, rims, stopper, and handle; Blank: crown, two shields, Vienna, Austria; ca. 1905–1925; $300–400.

After this course, the hostess signaled that dinner had ended. This could be accomplished by glancing in a significant way at the lady seated to the host's right that it was time to retire to the parlor, or by the hostess pushing back her chair. When the ladies withdrew, they were escorted by the gentleman with which they were initially paired. The ladies gathered in the parlor for coffee and liqueurs, while the men remained at the dining table or assembled in the library, finally free of conversation restrictions, ready to discuss business and politics while consuming their share of coffee and liqueurs, cigars, and cigarettes.

Cultivating Coffee and Culture

Coffee was a more popular drink in the United States, where Americans consumed four times as much coffee as tea by the mid-nineteenth century. In response to its popularity, coffee services, which also included a teapot as well as a sugar bowl, cream pitcher, matching cups and saucers, and trays, were produced in large numbers beginning in the 1880s.

Coffee pots are derived from the early English tankard, which was first used to serve coffee. A low hole was placed on the side opposite the handle, and a rounded, S-shaped pipe inserted into it. This is why coffee pots always are taller than teapots.

Tiny demitasse cups were reserved for after dinner, where coffee, thought to aid digestion as well as conversation, was served black and liberally sweetened with sugar in the French manner known as *café noir*. "Sugar is passed by a servant, or else the hostess drops two or three lumps of it in each saucer, a sugar bowl, with sugar

Four-piece coffee set; tray, 11"w by 7⅜"d; Burnished gold borders, rims, handles, and spout; Blank: T & V rectangle, Limoges, France; ca. 1919-1930; $150-200.

As a result of the British tea tax and the infamous Boston Tea Party of 1773, to this day Americans prefer coffee to tea. But almost a thousand years before this incident, coffee was cultivated in the Middle East. It was initially consumed as a food in parts of Africa around 800 A.D. Its use as a beverage was first recorded around 1000 A.D. by an Arabian philosopher and physician named Avicenna.

Coffee's stimulating effects were recognized early on. Originally limited to medicinal uses, it wasn't until the sixteenth century that coffee became a sociable drink in Arabia and Persia. There, Mohammedans took to drinking coffee instead of wine because of religious beliefs. The first coffeehouses, as recorded, were opened at Constantinople in 1554 by two merchants, Hakeem of Aleppo and Jems of Damascus. They were called *Mekteb-i-irfan,* which translates as "schools of the cultured," for coffee and intellectual discussions have gone hand in hand from the beginning.

The first coffeehouse opened in Oxford, England, in 1650. Continuing in the tradition of its Turkish homeland, English coffeehouses also became "schools of the cultured" because dons and students met there. Patrons came to sample the new, hot, and stimulating (but not intoxicating) drink. A few years later a coffeehouse was established in London, and by 1700, there were more than a thousand located in London alone! Boxes labeled "To Insure Promptness" were placed on walls for patrons to drop coins intended to speed the service of their waiter, and from this the word "tip" was coined.

Coffeehouses, which were a cross between a club and a tavern, were male bastions that attracted writers, artists, and other educated individuals. Merchants, too, found coffeehouses convenient places for business transactions. Real estate, commodities, and art objects were auctioned in salesrooms that were attached to coffeehouses. The great auction houses of Sotheby's and Christie's began in this way.

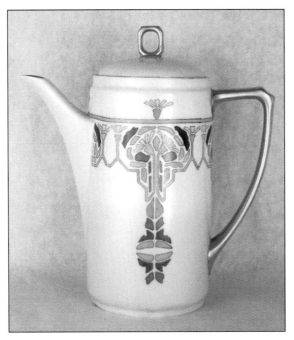

Coffee pot; 10"h (holds 48 oz.); Conventional-style design and ground colors executed in overglaze paints; burnished gold rims, spout interior, upper lip, and handles; Signed: "M. Larmour"; Blank: J & C, Bavaria; ca. 1902; $125-225.

Coffee pot; 8⅜"h (holds 24 oz.); Conventional-style dragonfly and plant executed in overglaze paints; iris and mother-of-pearl luster grounds; burnished gold border bands, rims, handle, and knob; Signed: "Lucille Long"; Blank: crown and shield, P.A., Arzberg, Bavaria; ca. 1927; $100-$175.

Individual coffee pot; 5½"h (holds 8-10 oz.); Conventional-style flower and ground color exectued in overglaze paints; burnished gold spout rim, handle tip, and knob; Signed: (illegible); Blank: Royal wreath, O. & E. G., Austria; 1909; $65-95.

tongs, standing beside her. Cream is not the correct thing for after-dinner coffee," wrote Cooke in *Our Deportment*. Afternoon coffee cups were similar in size to those we use today.

Instant coffee was created in 1906 and perfected in 1938. This, coupled with the invention and marketing of electric percolators beginning in 1908, condemned porcelain coffee pots as cabinet pieces. (Perhaps this hasn't been such a negative thing, for coffee pots often are found in mint condition.) Although brewed coffee has made a comeback today, thanks to drip coffeemakers and specialty shops that cater to this market, people are more likely to serve it from glass pots or plastic thermal carafes and drink it from practical microwaveable mugs.

In our streamlined lifestyles pouring brewed coffee into porcelain pots would mean one more object that required washing, and using cups and saucers would demand quite a balancing act from people rushing around in the morning! Additionally, saucers, which originally

After dinner coffee cup and saucer; Violets and ground color executed in overglaze paints; burnished gold handle; Signed: "Attai M Smith"; Blank: Circle, HR, Bavaria; ca. 1887; $25-35.

After dinner coffee cup and saucer; Wild roses and ground colors executed in overglaze paints; burnished gold border, base, rims, and handle; Signed: "To Y. Bencze, From M. Ritchie, 12-25-43"; Blank: none; $15-25.

After-dinner coffee cup and saucer; Roses and ground colors executed in overglaze paints; burnished gold trim, scrolls, and rims; Signed: "KGP, 1900"; Blank: France; $25-35.

served as a coaster to protect tabletops from being ruined by damp-bottomed cups, no longer are necessary for plastic laminate surfaces found in most kitchens.

Antique porcelains still can be employed for special occasions. Coffee pots may be safely used because coffee, which is acidic, usually does not come into contact with painted surfaces. However, bear in mind that coffee, as well as tea, may leach lead from hand painted china cups!★

★*For more information about possible lead poisoning from ceramic sources, see "Is Your Antique Dinnerware Dangerous?" at the end of this chapter.*

Coffee cups came in several sizes. Breakfast cups (right) held one and one-half cups of liquid. Afternoon coffee/tea cups (center) held 6 fluid ounces, similar to those we use today. In comparison, tiny demitasse cups (left) held one-third of a cup of rich black coffee. It was liberally sweetened with sugar in the French manner known as *café noir*.

Closing Time

After about twenty minutes, the men rejoined the ladies in the parlor. A nightcap of Crême de Menthe was offered to all guests. The final departure took place within thirty to forty-five minutes, but no later than eleven o'clock.

The custom of taking coffee and liqueur in the parlor, and later, the living room, remained convention as the twentieth century progressed. Eventually, the final dessert course was included, consumed in the living room or library. Ruth Berolzheimer, editor of *The American Woman's Cook Book* published in 1940, explained this custom as follows: "The original reason was to give guests more freedom and more luxury—dining-room chairs are stiff at best . . . . Besides, in many American homes, servants come in by the day or the hour. Serving coffee in the living room, in addition to the comfort it gives host and guests, allows maids to finish the cleaning-up process with more speed and care as well as more freedom. . . . In the maidless home, the dining-room doors can be closed, the lights turned out and both hostess and guests forget the work that awaits the former, in the glow of the larger, more comfortable and less formal living room." In fact, coffee tables, which are 17- to 19-inch high tables placed in front of sofas, are a twentieth century invention, created to facilitate this new routine. Likewise, tea tables came into being when the vogue for tea drinking in the mid-eighteenth century necessitated lightweight portable tables. Tea tables had round tops, and were about 20 inches high.

Ambiance is Everything

The dining room of today is apt to have limited use, even though it still contains the most expensive furniture. It is ironic how little this room gets used for actual dining. Businesses are launched here, homework projects accomplished, and even laundry folded. Fine dining is limited to holiday meals. In some social circles dinner parties are still vogue, but for the average family, dinner parties are a rarity. Entertainment and social events occur outside the home, or at informal get-togethers, such as barbecues and buffets, where eating occurs in the kitchen or on a patio.

Despite its lack of use, no homeowner would consider building a house without a dining room for resale and aesthetic reasons. Whereas once this room was located behind the parlor, generating a sense of visual surprise when guests first entered, modern floor plans place the dining room in the front part of a home so that passers-by get a glimpse of its fancy chandelier. In reality, the significance of the room has not changed in a century, for the dining room still registers the financial success, social status, and good taste of the homeowners.

Is Your Antique Dinnerware Dangerous?

New concern about lead poisoning from ceramic sources have caused many to question the safety of using their antique hand-painted tableware. Though glazed porcelain is vitreous (i.e., glass-like) and non-porous, long-term use and cleaning products may wear away any glaze, making it possible for lead to leach through.

According to Sandra Spence, executive director of the Society of Glass and Ceramic Decorators, this concern can be traced back to the early 1980s. A couple had collected hand-painted mugs from all over the world during their travels as military personnel. They would consume their morning coffee from a different mug each day. Coffee, being acidic, leached lead from these cups and over time, caused them to suffer from lead poisoning.

Beverages, such as coffee and tea, are more likely to leach lead, as are highly acidic substances such as citrus, tomatoes and tomato-based products, cola-type soft drinks, applesauce and apple juice, and salad dressings made with vinegar. Additionally, the composition of each mineral color varies, which in turn, affects its lead release level. Some hand-painted porcelain may have been underfired, making them more susceptible to releasing lead. Earthenware and other soft-glaze crockery tend to cause the most problems because of their porousness. Products from countries such as Mexico and China tend to be suspect, too, because their quality control standards are lax. However, high-fire glazes, such as those used in the production of porcelain, usually seal the glaze.

If lead were leached from china and ingested, because of the minute amount involved, it would be undetectable by taste or smell. Its symptomatic manifestations depend upon one's age, the amount of lead ingested, and the length of exposure. Symptoms associated with lead poisoning are nonspecific, making early diagnosis difficult. Serious cases of lead poisoning may cause gastrointestinal problems, lethargy, irritability, headaches, dizziness, numbness, and even kidney failure. Some may develop an anemia that mimics iron deficiency.

Knowing what we do today, was lead poisoning a problem for those who owned hand-painted porcelain tableware? It is reasonable to say that probably it was not. For example, decorations consisting of small floral bouquets actually left much of a vessel's surface undecorated. Additionally, expensive hand painted porcelain tableware was probably limited in use, put into service only when company came, and for special occasions.

In antique hand-painted porcelains, the basic ingredients of overglaze paints have remained virtually unchanged since its invention in China during the reign of Emperor Chenghua (1465-1487). These included the use of cadmium and lead. Therefore, is it safe for you to use your antique tableware? If you use pieces only occasionally, the answer is probably yes. *However, this author does not endorse the safety or use of hand-painted porcelain.* It is up to the individual to have porcelains tested, or to exercise caution and good judgment if choosing to use hand painted porcelains. Because of their susceptibility, pregnant women and children must be particularly cautious.

According to the Environmental Defense Fund, a national, not-for-profit organization dedicated to finding practical solutions to today's environmental problems, truly dangerous pieces of china are fairly rare. To be absolutely sure of the safety of using your antiques, however, have your tableware tested for lead. Spence questions the accuracy of lead-check tests which are available at hardware stores, though she agrees that tests from specialized laboratories are more costly. One company that was contacted quoted a price of 40 dollars for one sample submitted by a consumer, perhaps a small price to pay for peace of mind.

The Future of China Painting Products

The concern over lead in ceramic and ceramic decorating products has resulted in the trend towards the removal of lead and cadmium from these materials. Today china painters can choose from a wide range of lead-free colors that are bismuth- or zinc-based, though zinc-based colors are less durable. Lead-free paints are smoother and creamier because they are almost grit-free, but they may not develop the high sheen that occurs with leaded colors. Only some colors, such as yellows, oranges and fire reds, are less brilliant. To avoid contamination, however, china painters must use separate brushes and cleaner for lead-free paints.

There is a paradoxical dilemma concerning the utilization of these new paints. Jon Rarick, president of Trans World Supplies, Inc., manufacturers of china and glass paints and supplies, points out that bismuth- and zinc-based systems will leach lead from glaze unless the glaze is lead-free. Therefore, the replacement of lead-based paints does not solve the potential problem of lead leaching. Most glazed porcelain whiteware manufactured today has a low lead content, falling within acceptable U.S. Food and Drug Administration (FDA) ranges.

Mike McGuire, president of Mr. & Mrs. of Dallas, an importer of porcelain and glass and their decorating supplies, offers lead-free china colors in addition to their regular line of paints. McGuire says that it is unlikely lead-based paints will be completely phased out because a lot of porcelain remains decorative in purpose.

In 1994, the FDA issued final regulations concerning the labeling of ceramicware which could be used for storing or serving food, even when not intended as such. The FDA requires ceramic products to be conspicuously labeled according to their regulations that the piece is not for food use, or that a hole be bored through the potential food-contact surface. In drinking vessels, china painters may choose to leave two centimeters of the lip and rim area undecorated to meet safety standards. However, the ruling is not retroactive. Consumers remain at risk to lead exposure from porcelains decorated prior to that time.

SGCD Testing Laboratories

ACTS Testing Labs, Inc.
James M. Kinney
25 Anderson Road
Buffalo, NY 14225
716/897-3300

Intertek Testing Services—Labtest
Jeffrey Lipko
40 Commerce Way, Unit B
Totowa, NJ 07512
973/785-3220

Argus Analytical, Inc.
Greg McKnight
235 S. Highpoint Drive
Jackson, MS 39213
601/957-2676

Chicago Spectro Service Lab, Inc.
Dick Goldblatt
6245 S. Oak Park Avenue
Chicago, IL 60638
773/229-0099

Monarch Analytical Laboratories
Jurij A. Silecky
349 Tomahawk Dr.
Maumee, OH 43537-1696
419/897-9000

Professional Services Industries, Inc.
Elizabeth Motley
850 Poplar St.
Pittsburgh, PA 15220
412/922-4000

Cerdec Corporation
Pamela Lucas
P.O. Box 519
Washington, PA 15301
724/223-5900

To obtain a free copy of the brochure "What You Should Know About Lead in China Dishes," send a self-addressed, stamped envelope to: Lead-Safe China Brochure, Environmental Defense Fund, P.O. Box 96969, Washington, DC 20090.

A MODERN LIBRARY. PEN DRAWING BY W. P. BRIGDEN.

Drawing of a library from the December 1894 issue of **The Art Amateur.** *(Photo credit: The Newberry Library, Chicago)*

"IT DOES NOT FOLLOW THAT BECAUSE BOOKS ARE THE
CHIEF FEATURE OF THE LIBRARY, OTHER ORNAMENTS
SHOULD BE EXCLUDED..."

The Art Interchange
December 1901

Chapter Eight

Male Order: The Library

The library was a status symbol, often a somber room with a distinct masculine air. Yet even here books gave way to bric-a-brac. Scattered throughout the room were porcelain bibelots for effect, use, and contemplation.

Double ink stand; 8³⁄₁₆"w by 4¹⁄₁₆"d; Mother-of-pearl luster ground; burnished gold rims, geometric design, and lids; Signed: "M.A.H. 1927"; Blank: chalice and circle, P.S.A.A., Bavaria; $50-75.

In the library the man of the house might retreat to do some "serious reading," which included books and periodicals on history and politics. Sitting at his desk to write some correspondence or balance accounts, he would use a quill pen, or after 1884, a fountain pen. These might be stored on a porcelain pen tray and filled from a porcelain inkwell. (Although the ballpoint pen was patented in 1888, it wasn't developed and marketed until 1938.) Or he could invite some other men to light up a cigar or cigarette, and share a drink or two.

Up in Smoke

Smoking was widespread among the Native Americans in the New World, and it is believed that tobacco—along with corn, potatoes, and tomatoes—was native to the Americas. Christopher Columbus and other traders brought tobacco back to European nations, where it was quickly embraced due to its novelty and addictive qualities. Spain, Portugal, and eventually England eagerly established colonial sources.

At the end of the eighteenth century, eighty percent of American tobacco production was centered in Virginia and Maryland. Developments in the tobacco plant and curing methods were partly responsible for the spread of tobacco growing to southern Ohio, southern Wisconsin, Kentucky, Tennessee, and Missouri during the 1800s.

In the beginning, tobacco was smoked in pipes. The earliest pipe smoking on record dates back to the end of the sixteenth century in England. Until the mid-nineteenth century, clay and porcelain were the only materials used for the bowl of pipes. Porcelain bowls had painted scenes featuring deer, portraits, religious symbols, and mottoes.

Mexican Indians smoked tobacco in cigarette form. Spanish conquerors spread this habit into Turkey and Russia, and finally back to Europe via soldiers returning from the Crimean War in 1853. The invention of the safety match by a Swede in 1855 also fueled the smoking industry.

A cigarette manufacturing machine was invented by Albert H. Hook of New York City in 1872, but it wasn't until 1882 that it became a commercial success. Cigarette smoking became the preferred form of smoking tobacco in the United States, and was socially acceptable for men.

After dinner the men might congregate in the library or smoking room if they did not remain at the dining table, while the women withdrew to the parlor. Not only was the odor of tobacco considered disgusting by the ladies, but splitting into groups of the same gender allowed the men to "talk shop." Smoking, like drinking, became rituals associated with this form of male socializing. It would be another four decades before smoking by women gained acceptance.

Ashtrays as we know them today were designed around 1887. These differed from the "ash pans" that were previously used. Ashtrays had rounded rests for cigars or cigarettes. Some had attached match stands to hold matchboxes, which became available after 1875. Tobacco jars, also called humidors, kept tobacco moist.

Ash tray with attached match stand; 5¼"sq by 3½"h; Mason symbols executed in overglaze paints and burnished gold; burnished gold rims, bands, and monogram; Signed: "E. Watson, Xmas, 1916"; Blank: crown, H & Co., Selb, Bavaria; $45-65.

Stands were designed to accommodate match boxes, which were created in 1875.

Match stand; 5¼"dia by 2¾"h; Conventional-style lady's slippers and ground colors executed in overglaze paints; burnished gold stand and rim; Signed: "Gordon 1914"; Blank: Germany; $45–65.

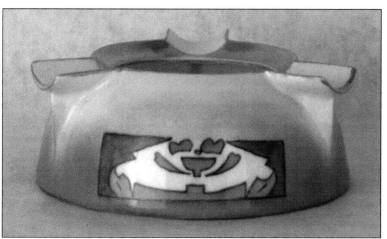

Ash tray; 3⅞"dia; Conventional-style floral and ground colors executed in overglaze paints; burnished gold rims and inside lip; Signed: "E.W. Misner"; Blank: Germany; ca. 1891–1914; $25–35.

Ash trays also were called "ash receivers" and "ash holders" in early china catalogs.

Tobacco jar; 5"dia by 7½"h; Geometric design executed in overglaze paints; burnished gold knob; Signed: "Convent, Key West, Fla."; Blank: T & V rectangle, Limoges France; ca. 1892–1907; $195–295.

A hand-painted porcelain smoking set was considered an appropriate holiday present. The article "China Objects for Decoration," which appeared in the December 1889 issue of *The Art Amateur*, stated:

"The china painter searching for something to decorate which will make a suitable present for a male friend will welcome the 'smoking set' just brought out. It consists of a tray holding a tobacco jar with cover, three open jars of sizes suitable for holding respectively, cigars, cigarettes and matches, and an ash tray. The whole thing costs only $1.25."

Liquor License

Along with offering cigars and cigarettes to his companions, a man might also offer some whiskey. Whiskey wasn't consumed in great quantity until after the American Revolution because the first whiskeys were harsh and expensive. Around 1800, improvements in distilling techniques led to a better brew, and in turn, increased consumption.

Eight-piece whiskey set; tray, 12"w by 8"d; Corn and ground colors executed in overglaze paints; burnished gold rims and handle; Signed: "SURQUIST"; Blank: jug, crown and two shields, Vienna, Austria; cordials, PP, La Seynie, Limoges, France; ca. 1903-1917; $300-400.

Jug listed as a grape juice jug in china catalogs published during Prohibition.

There were two types of whiskey that developed in the nineteenth century: corn and rye. Bourbon, which is made from corn, became the favored type of whiskey consumed in this country, and corn became a common motif on porcelain whiskey sets. These sets included a jug with six shot glasses, and a tray. They were at their height of popularity from around 1891 to 1929—even during Prohibition (1920 to 1933), when they remained as decorative ornaments, or were filled with homemade brews.

Downsizing

Houses became smaller as the twentieth century progressed. Men, women, and children had less space dedicated for their sole uses. The library, like the boudoir, and the nursery, disappeared as houses—and the servants required to maintain them—were downsized.

The average middle-class home built at the end of the twentieth century has enlarged from its predecessor of a half-century earlier. Floor plans often feature a fourth bedroom that is utilized as an office, and occasionally doubling as a guest room.

From his desk a man can pay bills without having to write a check, send an e-mail letter without having to pick up a pen, and read the day's headlines or a magazine without ever having to turn a page by using a desktop PC. He can chat over the Internet with people all over the world, without ever having been formally introduced, and without ever leaving home. This is his retreat, his equivalent of the library his ancestor once frequented to withdraw from his family.

"A MOTHER'S BEDROOM." DRAWN BY W. P. BRIGDEN. (FOR DESCRIPTION SEE THE OPPOSITE PAGE.)

Drawing of a mother's bedroom from the January 1895 issue of **The Art Amateur.** *(Photo credit: The Newberry Library, Chicago)*

"IN THE BOUDOIR WE SHOULD PREFER EVERYTHING TO BE
FAMILIAR AND HOMELIKE, AND TRUST FOR GRACE AND
HARMONY TO THE EXPRESSION OF ONE'S INDIVIDUAL TASTES."

The Art Amateur
June 1901

Chapter Nine

Feminine Retreat: The Bedroom and Boudoir

T he bedroom occupied by the master and mistress of the house was essentially a feminine room. Pale and serene hues and soft patterns enshrouded these rooms with an atmospheric ambiance that was contrasted by the massive, solid, and dark-stained furniture it contained. Personal touches provided by skilled hands gave the occupants private pleasures, and the room its personality. Dressers with split arms and shelves, dressing tables, and mantels provided places for the display and use of porcelain dresser sets, candlesticks, bud vases, and other decorative accessories.

Three-piece tea set (teapot holds 18 ounces); Burnished gold designs, handles, rims, and spout; Signed: "MSF"; Blank: Willets Belleek; ca. mid-1880s-1909; $250-400.

Three-piece tea set (teapot holds 18 ounces); Roses and ground colors executed in overglaze paints; burnished gold handles; Signed: "Louis"; Blank: Royal wreath, O. & E. G.; 1898-1918; $100-125.

Teapot and stand; Burnished gold bands, rims, spout, knob, handle, and stand; Blank: teapot, T V, Limoges, France; 1907-1919; stand, star, wreath, R. S. Germany; ca. 1904-1938; $50-75.

In the Victorian era, bedrooms functioned as more than places to sleep. A portion might be arranged as a boudoir—an intimate sitting room—where women ran their households, wrote letters, read, mended, relaxed, and sometimes entertained one or two of their closest friends. The lady of the house could offer her visitor a cup of tea from a small-size, intimate tête-a-tête porcelain tea set. This set included a two-cup teapot, creamer, sugar bowl, two cups and saucers, and a serving tray.

Not all homes were equipped with bathrooms, and many bedrooms contained washstands for daily cleaning and grooming. A commode set included a basin and pitcher, soap dish, cup, toothbrush holder, shaving mug, and chamber pot. China catalogs of the period did not feature commode sets, but china painters could decorate some of the smaller, individual items. The dressing area also could include a toilet table that held dresser sets and grooming items.

Chambersticks and Candlesticks

Candlesticks refer to the taller version of candleholders. These could be used on dining tables as well as dressing tables. Chambersticks were designed for bedrooms, although in china catalogs this style is called a candlestick as well. These were low candleholders with an attached tray. The ring loop for the insertion of fingers and the attached tray made it easier to carry the chamberstick from place to place without concern for dripping candlewax.

Match kettle; 2⅞"dia by 2½"h; Primrose and ground color executed in overglaze paints; burnished gold rim, handles, and feet; Blank: Germany; ca. 1891-1914; $30-45.

Candlestick; 6"dia by 2½"h; Violets and ground color executed in overglaze paints; white enamel embellishments; burnished gold rims, handle, and scrolls; Signed: "S. M. P."; Blank: T & V rectangle, Limoges, France; ca. 1892-1907; $40-55.

Dressed for Success

Dresser sets consisted of a tray to protect the surface of wooden furniture from scratching. Usually it contained a powder box, hair receiver, and jewelry box. Additional accessories included a pin tray, hatpin holder, ring stand, perfume bottle, talcum powder shaker, mirror, and one or two candlesticks. Accessories for men were limited to collar boxes, stickpin holders, pomade jars, and pin trays.

Five-piece dresser set: tray, 11"w by 7½"d; puff box; hair receiver; pair of candlesticks; Primrose and ground color executed in overglaze paints; burnished gold rims and feet; Signed: "Steve"; Blank: various manufacturers from France and Austria; ca. 1905-1925; $225-325.

Four-piece dresser set: candlestick, 5"h; hat pin holder, 4⅞"h; puff box; hair receiver; Conventional-style chickory design and ground color executed in overglaze paints; silver borders, top of candlestick, and top of hat pin holder; Blank: candle, T & V rectangle; puff box and hair receiver, Limoges scroll, W. G. & Co., Limoges, France; ca. 1900-1915; $150-225.

Two-piece dresser set: tray, 11½"w by 8¼"d; puff box; Roses and ground color executed in overglaze paints; burnished gold rim and knob; Blank: powder box, T & V rectangle, Limoges, France; ca. 1892-1917; tray, B & Co., Limoges, France; ca. 1914-1930s; $80-110.

Comb and brush tray; 11⅝"w by 8¹/₁₆"d; Double violets and ground colors executed in overglaze paints;
burnished gold rim and scrolled medallions; Signed:
"F. B. Hall"; Blank: T & V rectangle, Limoges,
France; $50-85.

Comb and brush tray; 13½"w by 8¼"d; Wild roses
and ground colors executed in overglaze paints; burnished gold rim and monogram; Signed: "K"; Blank:
T & V rectangle, Limoges, France; ca. 1892-1907;
$50-85.

Perfume bottle; 2½"dia by 4¾"h;
Wild roses and ground colors executed in overglaze paints; burnished gold rim; Blank: Limoges
scroll, W. G. & Co., Limoges,
France; ca. 1900-1932; $50-75.

Perfume bottle; 4¼"h;
Conventional-style florals and
ground colors executed in overglaze
paints; burnished gold border band
and stopper; Blank: Royal wreath,
O. & E. G.; 1898-1918; $50-75.

Perfume bottle; 5"h (missing stopper); Forget-me-nots, scrolls, and
ground colors executed in overglaze
paints; white enamel embellishments; burnished gold rim; Blank:
Royal wreath, O. & E. G.; 1898-
1918; $50-75.

Ring stand; 4½"w; Forget-me-nots and ground colors executed in overglaze paints; white enamel embellishments; burnished gold rim, scrolls, and hand; Blank: Royal wreath, O. & E. G.; 1898-1918; $35-50.

Ring stand; 3⅞"w; Etched and burnished gold violets; burnished gold rim and hand; Blank: T & V rectangle; ca. 1892-1907; $35-50.

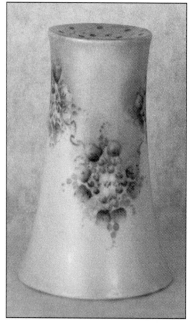

Talcum powder shaker; 5"h; Roses and ground colors executed in overglaze paints; burnished gold top and base; Signed: "M. Perl"; Blank: Favorite, Bavaria; ca. 1908-1920; $75-95.

Talcum powder shaker; 4½"h; Forget-me-nots and ground colors executed in overglaze paints; burnished gold top; Signed: "M.D."; Blank: none; ca. 1900-1950; $65-85.

Talcum powder shaker; 4¾"h; Forget-me-nots and ground colors executed in overglaze paints; burnished gold top; Stamped: "Stouffer" (Stouffer Studio, Chicago, 1906-1914); Blank: Royal wreath, O. & E. G.; $75-95.

Hand mirror; 10¼"w by 6⅛"d; Roses and ground colors executed in overglaze paints; brass frame; Blank: unknown; ca. 1890-1915; $100-150.

Pin tray; 5¼"w by 3"d; Forget-me-nots and ground color executed in overglaze paints; white enamel embellishments; burnished gold rim; Signed: "Harris"; Blank: crowned double-headed bird, MZ, Austria; ca. 1884-1909; $40-50.

Pin tray; 5¼"w by 3"d; Violets and ground colors executed in overglaze paints; burnished gold rim; Signed: "Sherratt" (Sherratt Studio, Washington, D.C.); Blank: T & V rectangle, Limoges, France; ca. 1892-1907; $40-50.

Pin tray; 5"sq; Tulips executed in overglaze paints; burnished gold border; Signed: "JRS"; Blank: none; ca. 1900-1915; $40-50.

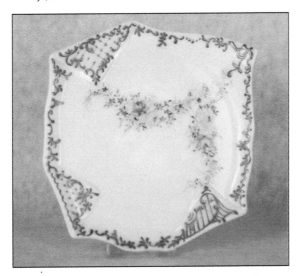

Pin tray; 4¾"sq; Floral garlands executed in overglaze paints; raised paste and burnished gold border pattern; Blank: Circle, Leonard (P. H. Leonard, New York City, importer); Blank: Vienna, Austria; ca. 1908; $40-50.

Pin tray; 5³⁄₄"w; Roses and ground colors executed in overglaze paints; burnished gold rim; Signed: (illegible); Blank: none; ca. 1900-1920; $40-50.

Pin tray; 3¹⁄₂"w; Violets and ground color executed in overglaze paints; burnished gold border and rim; Signed: "M. Burnet"; Blank: Royal wreath, O. & E. G.; 1898-1918; $18-25.

Hair Receivers and Hair Art

Victorian people remain well-known for their sentimental outlook. Hair was removed from brushes and stored in hair receivers. Eventually this hair was woven into pictures and jewelry that became treasured keepsakes expressing affection and remembrance. Actually, the practice of making ornaments out of human hair was not a new phenomenon when it reached its height of popularity in the mid-nineteenth century. As with so many forms of artistry, it, too, had its periods of popularity and of decline.

While the importation of European hair measured in the tons, and commercially woven products had sales reaching over a million dollars, nothing replaced the

Three-piece dresser set: pin tray, 5³⁄₄"w by 4¹⁄₁₆"d; hair receiver; puff box; Roses and ground colors executed in overglaze paints; burnished gold rims, bands, and knob. Stamped: "Julius H. Brauer" (Chicago, 1911-1926); Blank: Olimpic, Germany; $100-150.

Hair receiver, jewel table stand, and puff box; Roses and ground colors executed in overglaze paints; burnished gold scrolls and feet; Blank: crown, two shields, Vienna, Austria; ca. 1900-1920; $175-200.

sentiment of using the hair of a loved one. Additionally, accomplishing the art itself assured one that the locks of a loved one were employed and not unscrupulously substituted with a stranger's hair when given to a commercial weaver.

The task of preparing and weaving even simple jewelry pieces was no small feat, for human hair had to be boiled, sorted, bound, and weighted. Bobbins, used in lace making and tapestry weaving, also were employed in the art of hair weaving. Victorian hair workers wove jewelry in the simplest square chain braid, as well as elaborate pieces in open braids.

By the early twentieth century, the art of hair-work had fallen in popularity. Photography now provided sentimental keepsakes. Hair-work became regarded as old-fashioned and tedious, qualities eventually applied to the art of china painting, responsible in part for its demise. Despite the decline of hair-work as an artform, hair receivers continued to be offered as part of dresser sets. Perhaps this was out of practicality. Hair that was removed from brushes could be used to make hair rats. These were pads with tapered ends used in hairstyling beginning in the 1890s to give the appearance of greater volume. Loose hair also could be stored in the hair receiver until full, then emptied all at once into a trashcan.

Two-piece dresser set: hair receiver; puff box (with original puff); Roses and ground colors executed in overglaze paints; burnished gold knob and rim; Signed: "Al"; Blank: T & V rectangle, Limoges, France; ca. 1892-1907; $155-175.

Violet holder; Burley & Co.; Catalogue No. 19; ca. 1910.

Hair receivers and powder boxes were very similar. Both shared the same basic form and the same base. The difference was in their lids. Powder boxes had closed covers, usually with a handle at the top. Hair receivers had holes in the middle.

There also was a violet flower holder with the same base, but different lid. This holder had a large hole in the center of its lid like the hair receiver, but it was dotted with additional small holes.

Hatpins, Stickpins, and Incense Burners

At the height of the china painting movement, no woman ventured outside without her hat. These enormous and elaborate accessories were held in place by hatpins. Porcelain hatpin holders, measuring 4 to 6 inches high, safely stored sharp pointed hatpins. Its peak period of use occurred from 1890 to around 1925, when the close-fitting cloche made hatpins unnecessary.

Hatpin holders were part of dresser sets, but finding complete dresser sets in the antique marketplace is rare, for collectors are willing to pay as much as one-third the value of a set just for the hatpin holder! For example, hatpin holders are generally priced between seventy-five and ninety-five dollars, while dresser sets are valued between two-hundred-fifty to four hundred dollars, depending on the number of pieces and the decoration.

In an effort to stimulate sales, importers might come up with new uses for existing forms, which is exactly what the W. A. Maurer China Store did. This china distributor advertised the very same blanks as incense burners in the January 1922 issue of *Keramic Studio* magazine. Then, too, the owner of a decorated hatpin holder might have adapted it for this new purpose. There is no definitive way to target a holder's use, for had it held incense, its smoky fragrance has long since dissipated.

In the days before tie clips, men and women used stickpins to hold their scarves and ties in place. Stickpin holders, like hatpin holders, were employed to safely store the pins. They ranged from 1½ to 2 inches high, about the size of an individual salt and pepper shaker.

Hat pin holder; 4½"h; Wild roses and ground colors executed in overglaze paints; yellow enamel flower centers; burnished gold rim and top; Signed: "ARM"; Blank: none; ca. 1890-1914; $85-95.

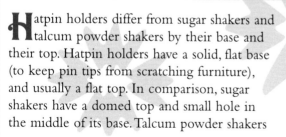

Hatpin holders differ from sugar shakers and talcum powder shakers by their base and their top. Hatpin holders have a solid, flat base (to keep pin tips from scratching furniture), and usually a flat top. In comparison, sugar shakers have a domed top and small hole in the middle of its base. Talcum powder shakers have a larger hole in the middle of their bases.

Hatpin holders have six to twelve pin-holes. A larger hole in the middle could accommodate hairpins and pin-ornaments with heavy shanks that would not fit into the smaller holes, as well as sheath-type corsage and scarf pins. Attached trays stored rings and small pins.

Stickpin holders also could have the same shape as a salt and pepper shaker. The size of the holes on top differentiates the two. Stickpin holders had larger holes than salt or pepper shakers, a comparison which becomes obvious when viewed side by side.

Stickpin holder; 3"h; Holly and ground colors executed in overglaze paints; burnished gold top; Blank: crown, pair of lions in shield; ca. 1915–1935; $10–25.

Collar Button Boxes

In the late nineteenth and early twentieth centuries men wore stiff, starched collars that were attached separately from their shirts. These collars were held in place by closures that were stored in collar button boxes. There was no mistaking a collar button box, for its appearance in porcelain was an exact reproduction of a man's shirt collar.

Shaving Mugs

Shaving mugs were another masculine article found in the bedroom, as well as the barber shop. A cake of soap was placed inside the mug. A wet shaving brush (which could have a hand-painted porcelain handle) was swirled around the soap cake to create shaving lather. Then the brush was used to apply the lather to a man's face.

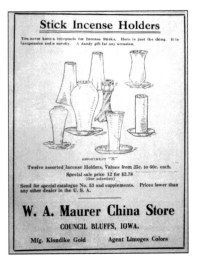

Advertisement in the January 1922 issue of **Keramic Studio.**

Shaving mugs varied from drinking mugs and tankards by their thickness, although one writer mentioned in an article in the June 1899 edition of *The Art Interchange* that adaptation sometimes was the result of overabundance:

"The output of shaving mugs, those perennial standbys of gift-giving womankind, will have to share the market with [whisky jugs and tobacco jars.] Let us be thankful. Man can not live with shaving mugs alone. He has been known to use them for beer mugs."

Shaving mug; 3¾"h; and shaving brush; Conventional-style design and ground color executed in overglaze paints; burnished gold border, band, and handle; Blank: Germany; ca. 1891-1914; $30-40.

Collar button box; 2½"dia by 1¼"h; Conventional-style floral design and ground color executed in overglaze paints; burnished gold knob; Blank: Germany; ca. 1892-1914; $15-25.

No Time for Contemplation

Today's bedrooms have diminished in size. Only larger homes of the wealthy may contain a separate sitting area off the master bedroom. It still remains a private retreat, but serves functions other than visiting, mending, or writing. Prior to succumbing to the swelling wave of slumber, couples may watch television or read, often while lying in bed.

Upon arising, morning ablutions are performed in a separate but attached bathroom, and dressing accomplished either in the bathroom or bedroom. If there is a dressing table at all, it is usually located in the bathroom, often part of the countertop with the bathroom sink. There may be a tray for perfume and cologne bottles, but gone are the fancy and functional porcelain accoutrements. Numerous items, such as powder boxes and talcum powder shakers, are obsolete. Cosmetics companies package their own talcum powders and some have produced perfume bottles that have become collectibles in their own right. Jewelry boxes are catchalls, eliminating the need for separate ring and pin holders.

Getting dressed in the morning has become a rushed process, one that makes no time for the contemplation of beautiful, utilitarian objects, such as hand-painted porcelains. American painted porcelain has become an endangered category of icons that symbolized a culture which equated useful items artistically embellished with an elevated existence and higher social class.

Appendix

Ascertaining the Functions of Antique China: Resources and References

*"Ceramics came about by chance, by intention,
and by invention."*
Mrs. Nicola de Rienzi Monachesi, The Art Interchange, *August 1901*

Building and documenting an assemblage of American painted porcelain requires research, cataloging, and maintenance to preserve their history. But where does one look to find the information that will unlock the identification puzzle? The pieces themselves—their shape, their size, and their decoration—provide only partial answers.

Cookbooks, etiquette books, books comprised of period interior photos, as well as historical fiction and diaries furnish crucial information and a better understanding of an era. Cookbooks contribute more than recipes. Many include sections on menus, table layout, service methods, and dinnerware. Etiquette books cover making calls as well as hosting an afternoon tea—how to set up the room, what to serve, and what to wear. Books that feature collections of old interior photographs show details of daily life and interior decoration.

China catalogs are another important source, particularly those that catered to china painters. These illustrate styles and classify items. They picture various groupings of porcelain pieces that form sets, including lemonade sets, shrimp sets, dresser sets, or smoking sets.

Magazines that dealt with china painting, such as *Keramic Studio*, and with interior decorating and lifestyle, such as *The House Beautiful* and *The Ladies' Home Journal*, are additional important resources.

Books particularly, and old magazines occasionally, can be found in antique shops and malls throughout the nation. More often, periodicals, as well as china catalogs, are more likely to be located through ads in specialty newspapers, such as *The Antique Trader* and *Warman's Today's Collector*, in magazines that deal with antiques, through people and businesses that specialize in this type of merchandise, and on Internet auction sites.

Sometimes periodicals may be available on microfilm, and some libraries have bound sets available for use on site. *The Art Amateur* is available on microfilm from the Library of Congress. The Newberry Library in Chicago has a nearly complete set of this magazine. The Milwaukee County Public Library, downtown facility, has a complete set of *Keramic Studio*, as does the Ryerson Library at the Art Institute of Chicago. (Museum membership is required to access the Ryerson, however.)

These and other libraries also have books on porcelain and china painting, many of which are rare or out-of-print. For example, the Milwaukee County Public Library has china painting books by Mary Louise McLaughlin, Henrietta Barclay Paist, Adelaide Harriett Osgood, and Mrs. C. C. Filkins. The Athenaeum of Philadelphia has a copy of the book *A Practical Treatise on China Painting in America, with Some Suggestions as to Decorative Art* by Professor Camille Piton of Philadelphia, whose works were featured in *The Art Amateur*.

Be forewarned that building a good working library, like building a decent collection of American painted porcelain, can be an expensive proposition. Etiquette books can cost as little as five dollars, while old cookbooks can cost up to twenty-five dollars. I've even paid as much as $125 for an out-of-print book. Price is not always dependent upon age. An out-of-print book that is less than ten years old may cost as much as one that is over one hundred years old. Demand determines the price.

Inter-library loan services can be utilized for the cost of a postcard stamp. It always amazes me how many truly old books are still in circulation. I've been able to borrow books dating back to the beginning of the century.

Issues of *Keramic Studio* average fifteen dollars. *The Ladies' Home Journal* can sell for as much as twenty-five dollars each. Owning complete sets of these magazines would require a major investment—if one could even locate a set for sale. Don't be discouraged, however. Even a handful of issues may furnish important revelations.

It requires imagination to think of objects in their relevant social and artistic context. Historical fiction and diaries bring readers into the proper mind frame that will allow them to visualize period room settings and scenarios. Sometimes these stories also can help date pieces and understand their uses. They might trace the origins of pieces and examine these objects within their particular culture and time period. Novels by literary masters such as Edith Wharton, William Dean Howells, and Henry James, many of which are still in print, are excellent references.

Historic homes, museums, and historical societies present settings for, and the placement of, porcelains, and contribute historical information about these pieces. Although few are devoted strictly to American painted porcelain, viewing all kinds of hand-painted pieces and their settings is essential for visual education. Below is a listing of some of these that feature American painted porcelain.

Museums

The Brooklyn Museum
200 Eastern Parkway
Brooklyn, New York 11238-6052
718/638-5000

The Brooklyn Museum has a large, rich, and varied hand-painted porcelain collection, including both factory and studio porcelain, documented and unattributed pieces. Because of the large size of the ceramics collections, not all pieces are on display.

The Cincinnati Art Museum
Eden Park Drive
Cincinnati, Ohio 45202
513/721-5204

The Cincinnati Art Museum has a rotating exhibit of Mary Louise McLaughlin's work, though not necessarily of her overglaze-decorated pieces.

Cooper-Hewitt
National Design Museum
Smithsonian Institution
2 East 91 Street
New York, New York 10128-9990
212/860-6868

An appointment is necessary to view pieces decorated by Edward Lycett, Laura Eckroth Lake, "Healy Gold" tableware gilded by the Healy sisters of Washington, D.C., and Caroline Virginia McGuffey when not on display.

The Metropolitan Museum of Art
1000 Fifth Avenue
New York, New York 10028
212/879-5500

Their collection includes thirteen pieces, mostly plates, some of which were decorated by well-known porcelain artists, such as Mary Louise McLaughlin, Anna B. Leonard, Maude Mason, and Clara Chipman Newton. They currently are on view in the Henry R. Luce Center, located in the American Wing.

Museum of the City of New York
Fifth Avenue at 103rd Street
New York, New York 10029
212/534-1672

The collection of the Museum of the City of New York includes the work of two china painters, Fanny Taylor Rowell and Lida Mulford (later Mrs. Charles Davies). According to their files, Rowell was awarded the Diamond Medal from the National League of Mineral Painters in 1898, and she authored a pamphlet entitled "The Use of Lusters." An appointment is necessary to view the porcelains painted by these artists.

Museum of Porcelain Art
International Porcelain Artists and Teachers, Inc.
204 E. Franklin
Grapevine, TX 76051
817/251-1185

This museum contains American and European hand-painted porcelain. Call for details.

The National Museum of American History
Smithsonian Institution
Constitution Avenue between 12th and 14th Streets N.W.
Washington, DC 20560
202/357-2700

Those who wish to view their collection of American painted porcelain may call the Division of Ceramics and Glass at 202/357-1786 for an appointment.

New Jersey State Museum
205 W. State Street, CN530
Trenton, New Jersey 08625-0530
609/292-6308

This museum has in its collection American Belleek china decorated by various factories, as well as independent artists and studios. A selection of pieces are on display in the Ceramics gallery.

Oakland Museum of California
Art Department
1000 Oak Street
Oakland, California 94607
510/238-3005 ext. 1059

This museum has in its holdings the china paintings of Helen Tanner Brodt (1838-1908). She was a professional artist and art teacher who at one time managed the entire art program for the Oakland school system. Her involvement with china painting lasted from around 1879 to 1885, at which time she received an award at the World's Industrial and Cotton Centennial Exposition held in New Orleans. Porcelain pieces consist of plates, cups, and teapots as well as drawings and paintings. Although only one piece is on display, an appointment can be made to view selected pieces in storage.

Pewabic Pottery
10125 E. Jefferson Avenue
Detroit, Michigan 48214
313/822-0954

Though none of Mary Chase Perry's porcelain artworks are housed here, her correspondence, sketches, and watercolor designs for china painting are. Research facilities and archives are open to the public by appointment.

Ross C. Purdy Museum of Ceramics
  at the American Ceramic Society
735 Ceramic Place
Westerville, Ohio 43081
614/890-4700

Two examples of Mary Louise McLaughlin's hand-painted porcelains are on display.

Sinsinawa Dominicans
Heritage Room
Sinsinawa Dominican Archives
Sinsinawa, Wisconsin 53824
608/748-4411

Susan Frackelton's daughter Gladys attended St. Clara Academy (Class of 1904) at Sinsinawa. On display is Frackelton's extraordinary hand-painted porcelain baptismal font, which received a medal at the 1893 Columbian Exposition in Chicago; a set of game plates, including a 16-inch charger; and samples of the china paints Frackelton manufactured. Also exhibited are porcelains painted by the sisters and students who taught, or attended, china painting classes held at the academy. An appointment is necessary to view the collection.

Strong Museum
One Manhattan Square
Rochester, New York 14607
716/263-2700

Margaret Woodbury Strong's collections comprise the core of this museum. Her mother, Alice Woodbury, had been a china painter. In all there are about 180 pieces of porcelain manufactured in the United States, and an equal amount of imported whiteware decorated by American artists.

World Organization of China Painters
Foundation Center & Museum
2641 N.W. 10th Street
Oklahoma City, Oklahoma 73107
405/521-1234

The main building consists of seven rooms, each housing antique and contemporary porcelain displays. Antique supplies and china paints, and a kerosene-fueled, Revelation-brand antique kiln, complete with instructions, are also exhibited.

Historical Homes

President Benjamin Harrison Home
1230 N. Delaware St.
Indianapolis, IN 46202-2598
317/631-1898

President Harrison's (1888-1892) first wife Caroline was a china painter who studied with Paul Putzki (see salts dips on page 94 and plates on page 144). Her sitting room on the second floor, adjacent to the master bedroom, was also her studio. Numerous examples of Caroline's painted porcelains are located throughout the home.

Juliette Low House
142 Bull St.
Savannah, GA 31401
912/233-4501

Juliette Gordon Low, founder of Girl Scouts, studied china painting with Edward Lycett when she was a student at Mesdemoiselles Charbonnier's school in New York City beginning in 1878. Housed in a china closet in the dining room are ten plates, all painted prior to 1885.

The McFaddin-Ward House
1906 McFaddin Avenue
Beaumont, Texas 77701
409/832-2134

Built in 1905-1906, this Beaux-Arts Colonial-style mansion once was home to Ida Caldwell McFaddin, and her daughter Mamie McFaddin Ward. Both mother and daughter, and Ida's sister Louise Caldwell Watts, were china painters. The home features porcelain they collected, as well as painted.

Historical Societies

Chicago Historical Society
Clark Street at North Avenue
Chicago, Illinois 60614
312/642-5305

Many pieces from the 1979 exhibit Chicago Ceramics and Glass belong to the museum. One room on the second floor houses a permanent exhibit of Chicago Arts and Crafts. One case is devoted to hand-painted porcelains executed by Chicago porcelain artists and studios. Porcelains will be periodically rotated.

Milwaukee County Historical Society
910 N. Old World Third St.
Milwaukee, Wisconsin 53203
414/273-8288

Located in a 1913 neoclassical building that was once a bank, this historical society has twenty pieces of Susan Stuart Goodrich Frackelton's painted porcelain, one of her paint sets, and several of her awards.

Minnesota Historical Society
345 Kellogg Boulevard West
St. Paul, Minnesota 55102
612/296-0150

American painted porcelains in their collection include a dresser set, a tea set, decorative plaque, vases, cups and saucers, and plates, as well as a paperboard study by Henrietta Barclay Paist. This collection is available for research by application and appointment with the Loan/Research Coordinator at 612/297-8094 or 8093. Two separate appointments are required for viewing artificats: the initial appointment involves reviewing the card catalog and photo file to select appropriate pieces; the second appointment is for actual viewing of the artifacts. Additionally, the second visit may require traveling to another facility.

Glossary

Abstract: An artistic style where forms are reduced to basic geometric components, often bearing little resemblance to the motifs on which the designs were based.

Acanthus leaf: A conventional representation of the leaf of the acanthus family, having three lobes.

Aesthetic Movement: A movement that reigned from around 1876 to 1890. Artists used nature for artistic models, and rendered their subjects realistically. Proponents of the movement also believed in making common objects beautiful artworks.

Arts and Crafts Movement: A movement popular from around 1890 to 1920. Proponents of this movement favored hand-crafted objects. Flat, geometric patterns characterize their decoration.

Art Deco: This style was popular in the United States from the mid-teens to well into the 1930s. Art Deco designs are characterized by pure geometry.

Art Nouveau: An artistic style fashionable from about 1890 to 1915. Art Nouveau designs are stylized abstractions of organic forms, usually of flowers and leaves. Characterized by sinuous, flowing lines, curves, and forms.

Backstamp: The porcelain manufacturer's mark, usually located on the base of a piece, identifying the factory, its location, and time period during which a piece of porcelain was made. Also called a mark.

Bar-le-duc: A fine and costly French red currant jelly.

Bibleot: A small object valuable for its beauty or rarity.

Biscuit: In British parlance, a cookie or sweet cracker.

Blanks: Undecorated, glazed white porcelain. Also called whiteware.

Boudoir: A woman's private sitting room, part of or adjacent to her bedroom.

Bouchée: Small pastry shells filled with creamed meat.

Bric-a-brac: Small, artistic objects or knickknacks placed throughout a room for decoration.

Burnish: To polish Roman gold after firing in order to bring out a soft sheen.

Cache-pot: The name cache-pot means "pot-hider." In Europe and England, terra cotta planters were meant to be placed inside cache-pots. The American term for this type of container was planter, although old china catalogs used the term "jardiniere."

Café noir: A strong, black coffee, served sweetened or unsweetened at the end of the dinner meal.

Canapé: Thinly sliced bread cut into small strips or circular pieces, that has been toasted, deep fried, or buttered and browned in an oven, and covered with a topping made from eggs, cheese, fish, or meat. Canapés may be served hot or cold.

Castor set: A set that contained a pair of cruets and other condiment containers, held within a frame or holder.

Chamberstick: These were low candleholders with an attached tray and a ring loop, allowing a person to carry the candleholder from place to place without concern for dripping candlewax. In period china catalogs, this style was called a candlestick, but varied from taller versions meant for stationary use on dining and dressing tables.

Charger: Chargers originally referred to large round or oval-shaped dishes that were used as meat platters. They were at least 12 inches wide. By the late Victorian era, chargers, which were called chop plates in china catalogs, were more likely to be used decoratively, rather than used as tableware.

China: Another name for porcelain, originally applied to porcelain imported from the country of China. Dinnerware made from various vitrified clay bodies also is called china.

China painting/china decorating: The fine art of decorating porcelain with various paints, metals, enamels, etc.

Chop dishes: Large dishes at least 12 inches in diameter. Decorated chop dishes were hung on walls and placed on shelves, rather than used as tableware.

Cloche: A style of close-fitting hat fashionable in the 1920s and 1930s.

Comport: A large dish, often elevated on a slender stem, used to serve candy, nuts, and fruit.

Compote: A dish used to serve a dessert made from cooked or fresh fruits and/or berries. It may be served in a rum, kirsch, or fruit bandy syrup.

Conventional style: Designs consisting of geometrical components rendered in flat or slightly modulated tones.

Cover: A place setting, usually consisting of the service plate, requisite silverware and glassware, and accessories such as salt dips and nut cups.

Croquette: A mixture of chopped meat, fish, or vegetables which has been coated with beaten eggs, rolled in crumbs, and deep fried.

Cruet: One-handled, narrow-necked bottles shaped like small decanters and sealed with a stopper. Used to store and serve vinegar and oil.

Decal: A form of mass-produced decoration where pictures and patterns are printed onto paper or plastic films, which are then applied to porcelain or pottery and fired. Mineral transfers were a form of decal.

Delftware, delft: A monochromatic style of painting, usually executed in grayish blue hues, depicting Dutch landscapes upon which the style is based.

Dinner: During the Victorian era, dinner referred to the mid-day meal, which is now called lunch.

Drawing/Withdrawing room: A term those in the upper class called their living room. Those in the middle classes called this room a parlor.

Enamel: A thick, opaque paste available in white and various colors, used to embellish paintings with dimensional effects.

Epergne: Fancy table centerpieces consisting of a combination of tiers of vases, candleholders, or dishes.

Étagère: An étagère was a larger version of the whatnot. It, too, featured graduated shelves beginning with the smallest at the top, but it was meant to be placed against a wall.

Ewer: Ewers are similar to cruets, but have wider necks and no stopper.

Firing: The process of baking porcelain and pottery in a kiln to harden clay, vitrify glaze, and mature decorations.

Flux: A glass paste (glaze) consisting of borax, flint, and lead and mixed with metallic salts to make overglaze paints.

Gilding: The application of gold to porcelain or pottery.

Glacéd: A candied or glazed coating.

Glaze: A colorless, thin coating of lead or alkaline, which may be mixed with feldspar. Glaze becomes smooth, hard, and translucent after firing, enclosing the clay with an impermeable layer of glass.

Hair receiver: Hair was removed from brushes and stored in a receptacle that resembled a puff box, but one which had a hole in the middle of its lid. The hair was saved for weaving jewelry and pictures, and later, for making hair pieces called rats.

Industrial Revolution: In nineteenth century America, the replacement of hand tools by machine and power tools, and the development of large-scale industrial production.

Jardiniere: Jardinieres were decorative planters that either had a hole in the bottom, or came with a pierced liner to provide drainage.

Jewels: Enamel decorations which simulate inset precious and semi-precious stones.

Loving Cup: A cup with three handles given as a token of esteem or affection. In large form, used as a vase.

Lusters: When fired, a mixture of metallic salts mixed with balsam of sulfur and thinned oil of turpentine that produces a lustrous and iridescent surface.

Marks: The porcelain manufacturer's identifying insignia, either printed, stamped, or hand-drawn. Usually located on the base of a piece. Marks assist in identifying the factory, its location, and the date of porcelain manufacture. Also called a backstamp.

Matt paints: Overglaze paints which lack flux, leaving a dull, velvet-like, opaque surface when applied on porcelain surfaces and fired.

Medium: Any artistic material or technique, such as watercolors, lithography, china painting, etc.

Mineral colors: Overglaze paints derived from metallic salts and combined with flux to render the colors fusible when fired at temperatures over 1,350 degrees Fahrenheit.

Mineral transfers: Vitrifiable decals printed with mineral colors from lithographic stones onto a paper back, used in the decoration of china.

Naturalistic style: A style of painting that portrayed natural subjects in a realistic manner, including their natural quirks, such as torn leaves and turned petals.

Overglaze paints: Glass paste (flux) colored with metallic salts. Also called mineral colors.

Overmantel: Towering shelving arrangements that rose vertically above the mantel shelf solely for the exhibition of ornamental objects, such as candlesticks, plates, and vases.

Parlor: A formal sitting room for the entertainment of guests, and sometimes family room as well.

Pelmet: A decorative cornice or valence at the top of a window which conceals drapery hardware.

Porcelain: There are two types of porcelain: hard-paste, or true porcelain, and soft-paste, or artificial porcelain. Hard-paste porcelain is a semi-vitified mixture of china clay (kaolin) and china stone fired at high temperatures (2,280° to 2,370° F) to create a translucent, bright white, and strong clay body. Soft-paste porcelain is a compound of white clay mixed with glass. It contains no kaolin.

Raised paste: A thick, opaque paste that was employed only as a basis for gold application. Used for three-dimensional effects.

Ramekin: An individual baking dish similar to a custard cup. Usually had a matching plate.

Ring stand: A flat dish with a hand or branch-shaped spine connected to its center. Used by a woman to hang her rings.

Rissole: A small ball of minced meat or fish, bread crumbs and egg, enclosed in a thin pastry and fried.

Rococo: An artistic style characterized by delicate scrolling and ornamentation imitating foliage.

Salt and pepper dredge: On September 15, 1863, a patent for a salt and pepper shaker as we know them today was granted. Originally this item was called a salt and pepper dredge, because the word "dredge" means "to sprinkle."

Salt dip: A small serving dish that held salt.

Saltcellar: A small dish for serving salt at the table.

Sugar shaker: Came into use in the last quarter of the nineteenth century. Sugar shakers were used for scattering caster sugar—a fine type of sugar resembling powdered sugar—and later cinnamon, over cake or fruit. Also called sugars.

Supper: In Victorian times, supper was the last meal of the day, now called dinner.

Sweetbread: The thymus gland of a calf that is parboiled, then broiled, re-heated in a sauce, sauteed, or fried.

Tabletops: Serving trays.

Transom: A small window or opening directly over a door.

Trencher: A tall salt dish with a scooped center.

Twelfth Night: The twelfth day after Christmas (January 6), when the Christmas season officially ended. A party was commonly held on this day that was called "Twelfth Night."

United States Centennial Exposition: An exhibition held in Philadelphia from May 10 to November 10, 1876, celebrating the nation's one hundredth birthday. Thirty-five nations participated, displaying machinery, industrial arts, inventions, and fine and decorative arts, spread throughout over 250 buildings.

Vitreous: Characteristic which exhibits a glass and waterproof surface.

Vitrine: A glass-enclosed cabinet for the display of art objects, curios, etc.

Whatnot: The whatnot was a triangular-shaped, open set of shelves usually made of mahogany, black walnut, or rosewood, and embellished with fretwork. The shelves graduated in size, beginning with the smallest at the top. Meant to fit into a corner, it could be either freestanding or wall-hung.

Whiteware: Undecorated, glazed white porcelain. Also called blanks.

Selected Bibliography

Categories of Porcelain Objects and Books Related to Their Function

Baker, Lillian. *Baker's Encyclopedia of Hatpins & Hatpin Holders.* Atglen, Pa.: Schiffer Publishing Ltd., 1998.

Baker, Lillian. *Hatpins and Hatpin Holders.* Paducah, Ky.: Collector Books, 1995.

Blake, Brenda C. *Egg Cups: An Illustrated History and Price Guide.* Marietta, Ohio: The Glass Press, Inc., 1995.

Campbell, Mark. *The Art of Hair Work.* 1875. Ed. Jules & Kaethe Kliot. Berkeley, Calif.: Lacis Publications, 1989.

Everyday Collectibles: China. Intro. Anthony Curtis. London: Chartwell Books, Inc., 1990.

Forrest, Tim. *The Bulfinch Anatomy of Antique China & Silver.* Consulting ed. Paul Atterbury. Boston: Little, Brown and Company, 1998.

Mace, O. Henry. *Collector's Guide to Victoriana.* Radnor, Pa.: Wallace-Homestead Book Company, 1991.

National Toothpick Holder Collector's Society. *Toothpick Holders: China, Glass and Metal.* Marietta, Ohio: Antique Publications, 1992.

Peterson, Arthur G. *Salt and Salt Shakers.* Washington, D. C.: Washington College Press, 1960.

Reader's Digest Treasures in Your Home. London: The Reader's Digest Association Ltd., 1993.

Revi, Albert Christian, ed. *The Spinning Wheel's Complete Book of Antiques.* New York: Grosset & Dunlap, 1972.

Wanvig, Nancy. *Collector's Guide to Ashtrays.* Paducah, Ky.: Collector Books, 1997.

China Painting—History and Process

Campana, D. M. *The Teacher of China Painting.* 10th Rpt. By the author, 1950.

The China Painter Instruction Book. Chicago: Thayer & Chandler, 1914.

Darling, Sharon S. *Chicago Ceramics & Glass: An Illustrated History from 1871 to 1933.* Chicago: Chicago Historical Society, 1979.

Filkins, Mrs. C. C. *The China Painters A-B-C.* By the author, 1915.

How to Apply Royal Worcester, Matt, Bronze, La Croix and Dresden Colors to China. 5th rev. ed. New York: Osgood Art School, 1891.

Kamm, Dorothy. *American Painted Porcelain: Collector's Identification & Value Guide.* Paducah, Ky.: Collector Books, 1997.

Kaplan, Wendy. *The Art that is Life: The Arts & Crafts Movement in America, 1875-1920.* Boston: Little, Brown and Company, and Museum of Fine Arts, 1987.

The Ladies, God Bless 'Em: The Women's Art Movement in the Nineteenth Century. (Exhibition Catalog.) Cincinnati: Cincinnati Art Museum, 1976.

McLaughlin, M. Louise. *The China Painters' Hand Book.* The Practical Series I. Cincinnati: By the Author, 1917.

McLaughlin, M. Louise. *Suggestions to China Painters.* Cincinnati: Robert Clarke & Co., 1884.

Monachesi, Mrs. Nicola di Rienzi. *A Manual for China Painters*. Boston: Lothrop, Lee & Shepard Co., 1907.

Paist, Henrietta Barclay. *Design and the Decoration of Porcelain*. Syracuse, N.Y.: Keramic Studio Publishing Company, 1916.

Phillips, L. Vance. *Book of the China Painter*. 1896. Rpt. by G. Burbank, 1969.

Wood, Serry. *Hand-Painted China*. How-to-do Section by S. S. Frackelton. Watkins Glen, N.Y.: Century House, 1953.

Cookbooks

Anyone Can Bake. New York City: Royal Baking Powder Co., 1928.

Berolzheimer, Ruth, ed. *The American Woman's Cook Book*. Chicago: Consolidated Book Publishers, Inc., 1940.

Buckeye Cookery and Practical Housekeeping. Rev. ed. Minneapolis, Buckeye Publishing Company, 1880.

Clark, Morton Gill. *A World of Nut Recipes*. New York: Avenel Books, 1967.

Farmer, Fannie Merritt. *The Original Boston Cooking-School Cook Book*. 1896 Facsimile. Hugh Lauter Levin Associates, Inc., 1996.

Glover, Ellye Howell. *"Dame Curtsey's" Book of Party Pastimes for the Up-to-Date Hostess*. 2nd ed. Chicago: A. C. McClurg & Co., 1912.

The Good Housekeeping Cook Book. New York: Farrar & Rinehart, Inc., 1943.

Howard, Maria Willett. *Lowney's Cook Book*. Rev. ed. Boston: The Walter M. Lowney Co., 1912.

Katz, Carol. *The Berry Cookbook*. New York: Butterick Publishing, 1980.

King, Caroline B. *Victorian Cakes*. 1941. Intro. Jill Gardner. Berkley, Calif.: Aris Books, 1986.

Lincoln, Mrs. D. A. *Boston Cooking School Cook Book*. 1887. Intro. Janice Bluestein Longone. Mineola, N.Y.: Dover Publications, Inc., 1996.

Marshall, A. B. *Ices Plain and Fancy*. Rpt. of *The Book of Ices*, 1885. Intro. Barbara Ketcham Wheaton. NY: The Metropolitan Museum of Art, 1976.

New York Herald Tribune Home Institute, comp. *America's Cook Book*. NY: Charles Scribner's Sons, 1942.

School of Domestic Arts and Science, comp. *Secrets of Correct Table Service*. Chicago: The Pickard Studios, 1911.

Townsend, Mrs. Grace. *Imperial Cook Book*. Rev. ed. Philadelphia: Elliott Publishing Co., 1894.

Wallace, Lily Haxworth, ed.-in-chief. *The New American Cook Book*. New York: Books, Inc., 1942.

Wild, Antony. *The East India Company Book of Chocolate*. London: HarperCollins Publishers, 1995.

Ziemann, Hugo and Mrs. F. L. Gillette. *The White House Cook Book*. Facsimile. (Orig. pub. 1887.) New York: Smithmark Publishers, Inc., 1995.

Culture

Beard, Lina and Adelia B. Beard. *The American Girls Handy Book*. 1898. Fore. Anne M. Boylan. Boston: David R. Godine, 1987.

Bok, Edward. *The Americanization of Edward Bok: An Autobiography*. Philadelphia: Charles Scribner's Sons, 1965.

Forty, Adrian. *Objects of Desire*. New York: Pantheon Books, 1986.

Garrett, Wendell D., et. al. *The Arts in America: The Nineteenth Century.* New York: Charles Scribner's Sons, 1969.

Green, Harvey. *The Light of the Home.* Asst. Mary-Ellen Perry. New York: Pantheon Books, 1983.

McClinton, Katharine Morrison. *Collecting American Victorian Antiques.* New York: Charles Scribner's Sons, 1966.

Schlereth, Thomas J. *Victorian America.* New York: HarperCollins Publishers, Inc., 1991.

This Fabulous Century: 1870-1900. Prelude. New York: Time-Life Books, 1970.

This Fabulous Century: 1900-1910. Vol. I. New York: Time-Life Books, 1969.

This Fabulous Century: 1910-1920. Vol. II. New York: Time-Life Books, 1969.

Etiquette

Ames, Kenneth L. *Death in the Dining Room.* Philadelphia: Temple University Press, 1992.

Cooke, Maud C. *Our Deportment, or the Manners and Customs of Polite Society.* Chicago: C. W. Stanton Company, 1902.

Eichler, Lillian. *Book of Etiquette.* Vol. 1. Garden City, N.Y.: Nelson Doubleday, Inc., 1923.

Gardner, Horace J. and Patricia. *Courtesy Book.* Philadelphia: J. B. Lippincott Company, 1937.

Hill, Thomas E. *Hill's Manual of Social & Business Forms: A Guide to Correct Writing.* Chicago: Moses Warren & Co., 1874.

Holt, Emily. *Encyclopaedia of Etiquette.* Vol. II. rev. ed. Oyster Bay, N.Y.: Nelson Doubleday, Inc., 1920.

Kasson, John F. *Rudeness & Civility.* New York: Hill and Wang, div. Farrar, Straus and Giroux, 1990.

Kingsland, Mrs. Burton. *The Book of Good Manners.* New York: Doubleday, Page and Company, 1904.

Northrop, Henry Davenport. *Golden Manual, or the Royal Road to Success.* Philadelphia and Chicago: International Publishing Co., 1891.

Post, Elizabeth L. *Emily Post's Etiquette.* 14th ed. New York: Harper & Row, Publishers, 1984.

Roberts, Helen L. *Putnam's Handbook of Etiquette.* New York: G. P. Putnam's Sons, The Knickerbocker Press, 1913.

History of Food and Dining Practices

Bartlett, Jonathon. *The Cook's Dictionary and Culinary Reference.* Chicago: Contemporary Books, A Tribune Company, 1996.

Chefetz, Sheila. *Antiques for the Table.* New York: Viking Studio Books, 1993.

Coe, Sophie D. and Michael D. Coe. *The True History of Chocolate.* London: Thames and Hudson, 1996.

Eskew, Garnett Laidlaw. *Salt: The Fifth Element.* Chicago: J. G. Ferguson and Associates, 1948.

Finch, Christopher and W. Scott Griffiths. *America's Best Beers.* Boston and New York: Little, Brown and Company, 1994.

Foster, Nelson and Linda S. Cordell, ed. *Chilies to Chocolate.* Tuscon, Ariz.: The University of Arizona Press, 1992.

Freeman, John Crosby. *Victorian Entertaining*. Philadelphia: Running Press Book Publishers and Michael Friedman Publishing Group, Inc., 1989.

Froman, Robert. *Man and the Grasses*. Philadelphia and New York: J. B. Lippincott Company, 1963.

Grover, Kathryn, ed. *Dining in America 1850-1900*. Amherst, Mass.: The University of Massachusetts Press; Rochester, New York: The Margaret Woodbury Strong Museum, 1987.

Kalman, Bobbie. *Food for the Settler*. The Early Settler Life Series. Toronto and New York: Crabtree Publishing Company, 1992.

Kane, Joseph Nathan; Steven Anzovin; and Janet Podell. *Famous First Facts*. 5th ed. New York: The H. W. Wilson Company, 1997.

Lovegren, Sylvia. *Fashionable Food*. New York: Macmillan (A Simon & Schuster Company), 1995.

Mariani, John F. *The Dictionary of American Food and Drink*. Rev. ed. New York: Hearst Books, 1994.

McGee, Harold. *On Food and Cooking: The Science and Lore of the Kitchen*. Collier Books. New York: Macmillan Publishing Company, 1984.

Paston-Williams, Sara. *The Art of Dining*. London: The National Trust, 1993.

Rhodes, Christine P., gen. ed. *The Encyclopedia of Beer*. New York: Henry Holt and Company, 1995.

Roberts, Patricia Easterbrook. *Table Settings, Entertaining, and Etiquette*. New York: The Viking Press, Inc., 1967.

Root, Waverly and Richard de Rochemont. *Eating in America*. Hopewell, N.J.: The Ecco Press, 1995.

Smith, Georgiana Reynolds. *Table Decoration: Yesterday, Today, & Tomorrow*. Rutland, Vt. and Tokyo: Charles E. Tuttle Company, 1968.

Tames, Richard. *Food: Feasts, Cooks & Kitchens*. New York and Chicago: Franklin Watts, 1994.

Tannahill, Reay. *Food in History*. New York: Crown Trade Paperbacks, 1988.

Trager, James. *The Food Chronology*. An Owl Book. New York: Henry Holt and Company, 1995.

Travis, Nora. *Haviland China: The Age of Elegance*. Atglen, Pa.: Schiffer Publishing Ltd., 1997.

Williams, Susan. *Savory Suppers and Fashionable Feasts*. New York: Pantheon Books, 1985.

Wise, William. *Fresh, Canned, and Frozen: Food from Past to Future*. New York: Parents' Magazine Press, 1971.

Visser, Margaret. *The Rituals of Dinner*. New York: Penguin Books USA Inc., 1991.

Home Design and Furnishings

Banham, Joanna; Julia Porter; and Sally Macdonald. *Victorian Interior Style*. London: Studio Editions Ltd., 1995.

Bowman, John S. *American Furniture*. New Jersey: Crescent Books, 1995.

Cirker, Blanche, ed. *Victorian House Designs*. Mineola, N.Y.: Dover Publications, Inc., 1996.

Cook, Clarence. *The House Beautiful*. 1881. Mineola, N.Y.: Dover Publications, Inc., 1995.

Delehanty, Randolph and Richard Sexton. *In the Victorian Style*. San Francisco: Chronicle Books, 1991.

Drury, Elizabeth and Philippa Lewis, comp. *The Victorian Household Album*. London: Collins & Brown, 1995.

Eastlake, Charles L. *Hints on Household Taste*. 1878. Intro. John Gloag. New York: Dover Publications, Inc., 1986.

Grier, Katherine C. *Culture & Comfort*. Washington, D.C.: Smithsonian Institution Press, 1988.

Grow, Lawrence and Dina von Zweck. *American Victorian*. New York: Harper & Row, Publishers, 1984.

Holly, Henry Hudson. *Holly's Country Seats*. 1863. Watkins Glen, N.Y.: American Life Foundation & Study Institute, 1980.

Leopold, Allison Kyle. *Victorian Splendor*. New York: Stewart, Tabori and Chang, 1986.

Lewis, Arnold, James Turner and Steven McQuillin. *The Opulent Interiors of the Gilded Age*. New York: Dover Publications, Inc., 1987.

Lichten, Frances. *Decorative Arts of Victoria's Era*. New York: Bonanza Books, div. Crown Publishers, Inc., 1950.

Miller, Judith and Martin. *Victorian Style*. London: Mitchell Beazley International Ltd., 1993.

Peterson, Harold L. *American Interiors: From Colonial Times to the Late Victorians*. New York: Charles Scribner's Sons, 1971.

Plante, Ellen M. *The American Kitchen: 1700 to the Present*. New York: Facts On File, Inc., 1995.

Plante, Ellen M. *The Victorian Home*. Philadelphia: Running Press Book Publishers and Michael Friedman Publishing Group, Inc., 1995.

Roe, F. Gordon, F.S.A. *Home Furnishing with Antiques*. London: Abbey Fine Arts, 1969.

Seale, William. *Recreating the Historic House Interior*. Nashville: American Association for State and Local History, 1979.

Seale, William. *The Tasteful Interlude*. 2nd rev. ed. Walnut Creek, Calif.: AltaMira Press, div. Sage Publications, 1995.

Wallace, Carol McD. *Victorian Treasures*. New York: Harry N. Abrams, Inc., 1993.

Wharton, Edith and Ogden Codman, Jr. *The Decoration of Houses*. New York: Charles Scribner's Sons, 1914.

Williams, Henry L. and Ottalie K. Williams. *How to Furnish Old American Houses*. New York: Bonanza Books, div. Crown Publishers, Inc., 1949.

Winkler, Gail Caskey and Roger W. Moss. *Victorian Interior Decoration*. New York: Henry Holt and Company, 1986.

Zingman-Leith, Elan and Susan. *Creating Authentic Victorian Rooms*. Washington, D.C.: Elliott & Clark Publishing, 1995.

Zingman-Leith, Elan and Susan. *The Secret Life of Victorian Houses*. Washington, D.C.: Elliott & Clark Publishing, 1993.

Home Economics

Beeton, Isabella Mary Mason. *Mrs. Beeton's Book of Household Management*. Rev. ed. London and Melbourne: Ward, Lock & Co., Limited, 1915.

Harris, Jessie W. and Elisabeth V. Lacey. *Everyday Foods*. Boston: Houghton, Mifflin Company, 1927.

Greer, Carlotta C. *Foods and Home Making.* Boston: Allyn and Bacon, 1928.

Morse, Sidney and Isabel Gordon Curtis. *Household Discoveries and Mrs. Curtis's Cook Book.* Petersburg, N.Y.: The Success Company, 1909.

Porcelain Artists, Studios and Marks

Lehner, Lois. *Lehner's Encyclopedia of U. S. Marks on Pottery, Porcelain & Clay.* Paducah, Ky.: Collector Books, 1988.

Reed, Alan B. *Collector's Encyclopedia of Pickard China.* Paducah, Ky.: Collector Books, 1995.

Romeyn, Carlyn Crannell, Ph. D. *The Lycetts.* Vol. 6. International Porcelain Art Teachers, Inc., 1983.

Weiss, Peg, ed. *Adelaide Alsop Robineau: Glory in Porcelain.* Syracuse, N.Y.: Syracuse University Press, 1981.

Articles

Brandimarte, Cynthia A. "Somebody's Aunt and Nobody's Mother: The American China Painter and Her Work, 1870-1920." *Winterthur Portfolio.* Vol. 23, No. 4 (Winter 1988), 203-224.

Stuart, Evelyn Marie, "America As A Ceramic Art Center," Chapter 11, Fine Arts Journal. (May 1910).

China Catalogs

Burley & Co., Catalog No. 19 (ca. 1910), Chicago

Thayer & Chandler, Catalog No. 58, 1909, Chicago

Thayer & Chandler, Catalog No. 96, September 1, 1919, Chicago

Thayer & Chandler, Catalog No. 99, February 1921, 1919, Chicago

Thayer & Chandler, Catalog No. 54, September, 1923, Chicago

Thayer & Chandler, Catalog No. 58, 1925, Chicago

W. A. Maurer, Catalog No. 70 (ca. 1923), Chicago

Maurer-Campana Art Co, August 1, 1929, Chicago

Periodicals

The Art Amateur, June 1879-September 1903

The Art Interchange, January 1892-January 1904

Crockery & Glass Journal, January 1877-December 1882; January 1899-June 1899.

The House Beautiful, June 1897-Nov. 1914

Keramic Studio, May 1899-April 1930

The Ladies' Home Journal, August 1984; July and October 1895; January 1896; June 1898; November 1906; September 1907; and November 1909

Abbreviations

h=height
d=deep
w=wide
dia=diameter
sq=square
ca.=circa

Alphabetical Listings of Artists and Studios

ARM 169

Al 168

Arkwright 77

Ashley, E.V. 60

ALB 130

E. B. 66

E. C. B. 41, 44

Bard (Isador Bardos, 1909) 43

Bawo & Dotter (New York City) 66

Beatrice (1907) 117

BENDER, N. O. 50

Betts, F. B. 80

Blake (1913-1916) 85

Brauer, Julius H. (Chicago, 1911-1926) 167

Breinin, Anne W. 51

Brentwood 82

Briccs, R. C. 133

Brown 91

Brown, A. 57

Burnet, M. 167

L. V. C. 47

S. D. C. (1904) 134

Carlson, Mabel (1917) 71

Carlyle (Margaret Carlyle, St. Paul, Minn.) 97

Chapman, R. F. 65

Chase, V. B. 124

Cliffe, J. M. (11/28) 113

Convent (Key West, Fla.) 157

C D (1878) 42

M. D. 165

Denison 83

Dorothy, M. H. 56

S. M. E. 118

Emma 36

H. B. F. 76

MSF 161

Louis F. 102

France, Robert W. (Chicago, 1906-1916) 73

France Studio (Chicago, 1906-1916) 73

Fritz, C. M. 67

AG 104

L. J. G. 94

M. G. (1929) 145

R. G. 138

GATES(?), M. 132

Gordon (1914) 157

Grech, E. 98

E. L. H. 106

M. A. H. (1927) 155

Hall, E. H. 105

F. B. Hall 164

Hanke, J. 134

Harris 166

Heap, S. (Samuel) (1906-1914) 77

Hey, F. L. 145

Heyn, C. (Charles Heyn, Chicago, ca. 1906-1916) 73

Hicok, M. L. 114

Hill, H. B. (Hazel B. Hill, Saratoga, N.Y., 1908-1915) 96

K 164

Kastner, F. (Milwaukee, Wis. 1912-1916) 100

Kayser's Studio, Milwaukee, Wis. (Mrs. Magdalena Kayser, ca. 1910-1915)s 42, 84

Keates Art Studios (Chicago, 1920-1937) 102

Keller, E. 99

Kendall, Maude 135

Kind 80

KISS, ALICE (Nov. 1920) 44

Kredell, Edith 42

Kreis (Carrie S. Kreis, Marion, Ohio, ca. 1901-1918) 101

KUMSTEAD, E. 97

C. L. (1901) 59

Larmour, M. 148

Laughlin 101

Lawer, E. W. (B29) 93

Leber, M J (1915) 37

Long, Lucille 148

Louis 161

Luken (Minnie A. Luken, Luken Art Studios, Chicago, 1895-1926)s 71, 135

Luman 96

Lycett, William (Atlanta, 1920-1938)s 60, 120

F. M. 137

M.E.M. 29

McCarthy, Schulz, Stuhl 136

McD 116

McGarry, A. W. (Amy W. McGarry, Cincinnati, 1897-1933) 96

McKee 135

McMiller(?), C. M. (Talladega, Ala.) 84

Merwin, Grace P. (Indianapolis) 86

MEYER 133

Miehling, B E (1899) 66

Miler, E. 47

Milne 136

Misner, E. W.s 43, 157

Mrs. Moore 81

Mueller, A. (1907) 75

Musselman 81

A. M. N. 82

Osborne 36

J. P. 35

KGP (1900) 149

L. R. P. (Jan. 1900) 69

S. A. P. 125

S. M. P. 162

Paddock, M. 118

Paine, Ida Lyston 118

Pasco 36

Patterson, C. N. (1908) 59

Pelton, Phoebe 139

Pep 102

Perl, M. 165

Pflaum, Louise M. 140

Pickard, W. A. (Pickard China Co., Chicago) 92

Pierce, A. E. 123

Pitkin & Brooks Studio (Chicago, 1903-1910) 98

Plachter, S. M. 133

Pugh, J. 133

Putzki, P. (Paul Putzki, Washington, D. C., ca. 1889-1915)s 94, 144

E. Q. 74

E. C. R. 93

F. M. R. (1899) 66

K. B. R. 36

L C R 78

Rhodes, F. C. (4-98) 79

Ritchie, M. (1943) 149

Rogers-Martini Co. (Chicago, 1913-1916) 85

Royal-Rochester Studios 137, 143

A. S. S. 130

E. M. B. S. 105

JRS 166

L. B. S. 121

Mill. S 83

R. A. S. 108

SANDWICH 62

Seybold 85

Sherratt (Sherratt Studio, Washington, D.C.) 166

Sitz, G. 91

Slocum 121

Smith, Attai M 149

Smith, Clara M. (ca. 1925-1928)s 38, 39, 40, 41

SmiTH, EdiTH 47

Sorenson, Olga (1904) 67

Sprecht, E. 34

Starer, E. 111

Steeberg, Mildred 138

Steele, Belle 101

Stenger, M. N. 47

Stephens, Charlotte (4/25) 51

Steve 163

R. STMD 43

STONER 75

Stouffer (Stouffer Studio, 1906-1914)s 43, 77, 80, 104, 165

Stuber, Mamie 87

Stupe, W. 85

SURQUIST 158

L. M. T. 82

Thonander, Chicago (John Thonander, 1910-1912) 37

Tolehard, C. E. (1914) 46

Tossys 94, 99

Townsend, J. 86

Tulmage, B. E. 44

L. V. 117

E. W. 41

FWFW (1910?) 43

L. V. W. (1903) 78

Walters 142

WANDS (William D. Wands, Chicago, 1910-1916) 125

Wats (Chicago, 1903-1910) 98

Watson, E. 156

WENTE, M. H. (1916) 50

White's Art Co., Chicago (ca. 1914-1923) 56

White, Claire 90

Wight, 79

Wigginton, M., 81

Wollastons 73, 108

Wright, Cora (New York City, ca. 1897-1907) 71

Yeazel 100

ZOOST, E. 135

Index

Aesthetic Movement 13, 21, 23

almonds 75, 132

The Art Amateur 20, 26, 30, 31, 32, 45, 46, 51, 64, 69, 83, 116, 141, 158, 160, 172, 173

Art Deco 15, 23

The Art Interchange 131, 142, 154, 170, 172

Art Nouveau 14, 67, 76

Arts and Crafts Movement 14, 23, 63, 76

bonbons 40, 43-45, 75, 117, 118, 119

bread and butter plate 45, 70, 100-103

butter, butter tubs 40, 98-100, 114

cake, cake plate 40-42, 45, 119

candlestick 67-68, 161, 162, 163

caster, caster set 108-109, 113

celery, celery set 119, 132, 134-136, 141

Centennial Exposition 10, 21

cereal, cereal bowl 111, 112, 113-114

charger 68, 69

cheese 40, 119, 141, 145, 146

cider 61

cigarettes 146, 156-158

cigars 146, 156, 158

coffee, coffee pot, coffee set 40, 58, 92, 111, 113, 119, 128, 146-150

conventional style, conventional design 14, 23, 24, 76, 87

crackers, cracker jars 40, 119, 130, 141, 146

Crockery & Glass Journal 72, 103

decals 18-19, 24-25

egg cup 111, 114-115

étagère 33

fern pots, ferneries 38-39, 65-66

fireplace 31, 32, 37-38, 39

game, game plate 87, 139-140

grape juice, grape juice jug 123-124, 158

honey 89, 113, 114, 119

hot chocolate 40, 56-58, 119

The House Beautiful (Clarence Cook) 32, 37-38, 63

The House Beautiful (magazine) 33, 64, 68, 73, 112, 172

ice cream 144-145

Industrial Revolution 22, 113

jardiniere 38, 65

jelly 112, 139

Keramic Studio 12, 24, 31, 63, 68, 69, 82, 87, 169, 170, 172, 173

The Ladies' Home Journal 63, 65, 127, 132, 136, 172, 173

lemonade, lemonade pitcher 40, 59-61

lily bowl 66-67

loving cup 65, 68

mantel, overmantel 37-38

maple sugar and syrup 114, 115-116

Morris, William 21, 23

napkins 70-71, 74, 103, 127

napkin rings 70-71

naturalistic style, naturalism 13, 24, 76, 87

nuts, nut dishes 75, 76, 117, 119, 125

oatmeal 113

olive 119, 125, 132-133

Paist, Henrietta Barclay 12, 24

pickles, pickle dish 118, 119

punch 40, 61-63

radishes 132, 141

ramekin 139, 141-143

Robineau, Adelaide Alsop 23, 24, 68, 69, 82, 87

salad, salad bowl, salad plate 69, 70, 139-141

salt dip 70, 94-95, 98

salt shakers 96-98

sardines, sardine box 131

soufflé 141-142

soup 119, 128-131

sugar 89-92, 115-116, 146

tea, tea set, tea table 40, 45-55, 56, 58, 92, 111, 119, 123, 125, 146, 147, 161-162

vitrine 21, 31

waterlilies 66-67

whatnot 21, 31, 32, 33

whiskey, whiskey jug 158, 170

World War I 23, 25, 92

World War II 103

About the Author

Dorothy Kamm is a noted award-winning porcelain artist, author, and expert on hand-painted porcelain. She received a B.F.A. from Northern Illinois University, where she graduated with University Honors and with Honors in English, and an M.F.A. from the School of the Art Institute of Chicago. She has written dozens of articles and lectured extensively on porcelain artistry and its history. In October 1992 she launched *Dorothy Kamm's Porcelain Collector's Companion,* a bimonthly newsletter covering antique hand-painted porcelain. Her first book, *American Painted Porcelain: Collector's Identification & Value Guide,* was published in June 1997. Her writings are on file in the library of the National Museum of Women in the Arts, the leading research facility on women's art.

Kamm, whose hand-painted porcelains were featured in *Victoria* and *Traditional Home* magazines, is a certified and registered artist and teacher by International Porcelain Artists and Teachers, Inc., based in Grapevine, Texas. She has been teaching the art of porcelain painting for more than a decade. Kamm was one of the founding members of the Treasure Coast of Florida branch of the National League of American Pen Women, two branches of American Association of University Women, the Benjamin K. Pierce chapter of Questers, a national organization dedicated to the study of antiques, and the Porcelain Artists of the Treasure Coast chapter of the Florida State Association of Porcelain Artists. Prior to pursuing a career in porcelain art, she practiced commercial interior design, taught college and adult art classes, and was associate editor of a design magazine. Kamm lives in Port St. Lucie with her husband and two daughters.

Antique Trader Books

we write the books on collectibles

{all kinds of collectibles}

Here are some of the books published by Antique Trader Books. For a complete list, please call 1-800-334-7165 and ask for a free catalog.

Collector's Value Guide To Oriental Decorative Arts • Sandra Andacht • AT5803 ....$24.95
Pottery And Porcelain Ceramics Price Guide, 2nd Edition • Kyle Husfloen, Editor • AT5730 ....$14.95
20th Century American Ceramics Price Guide • Susan N. Cox, Editor • AT5420 ....$14.95
American & European Art Pottery Price Guide • Kyle Husfloen, Editor • AT5412 ....$14.95
White Ironstone: A Collector's Guide • Kyle Husfloen, Editor • AT5366 ....$20.95
Collectible Glass Rose Bowls • A History and Identification Guide • Sean & Johanna S. Billings • AT0098 ....$26.95
50 Years of Collectible Glass, 1920-1970: Easy Identification And Price Guide • Tom & Neila Bredehoft • AT2579 ....$26.95
American & European Decorative & Art Glass Price Guide • Kyle Husfloen, Editor • AT5498 ....$15.95
Guide to Lace & Linens • Elizabeth M. Kurella • AT5897 ....$24.95
Monumental Miniatures • David Weingarten & Margaret Majua • AT2517 ....$28.95
Antique Trader's Antiques & Collectibles Price Guide 1999 • Kyle Husfloen, Editor • AT1999.............................$15.95
Antique Trader's Cashing In Your Collectibles • How To Identify, Value, And Sell Your Treasures • Miriam L. Plans • AT0039 ....$16.95
Caring for Your Antiques & Collectibles • Miriam L. Plans • AT5889...$15.95
Collectibles For The Kitchen, Bath & Beyond • Ellen Bercovici, Bobbie Zucker Bryson & Deborah Gillham • AT2520..........$21.95
Petretti's Soda Pop Collectibles Price Guide, 2nd Edition • Allan Petretti • AT0144 ....$29.95
Petretti's Coca-Cola Collectibles Price Guide, 10th Edition • Allan Petretti • AT5765...$42.95
American Tobacco Card Price Guide and Checklist • Robert Forbes & Terence Mitchell • AT5234 ....$29.95
Doll Makers & Marks • A Guide To Identification • Dawn Herlocher • AT004 ....$29.95
200 Years of Dolls Identification And Price Guide • Dawn Herlocher • AT5293 ....$17.95
Marionettes And String Puppets: Collector's Reference Guide • AT5943...$24.95
The Die Cast Price Guide, Post War: 1946 To Present • Douglas R. Kelly • AT5277 ....$26.95
America's Standard Gauge Electric Trains • Peter H. Riddle • AT5226 ....$26.95
Collecting Original Comic Strip Art • Jeffrey M. Ellinport • AT0101 ....$19.95
The Golden Age Of Walt Disney Records, 1933-1988 • R. Michael Murray • AT5706...$19.95
Tuff Stuff's Baseball Postcard Collection • A Comprehensive Reference and Price Guide • Ron Menchine • AT5536 ....$24.95
Mickey Mantle, The Yankee Years: The Classic Photography of Ozzie Sweet • AT5218...$39.95
Tuff Stuff's Baseball Memorabilia Price Guide • The Editor's of Tuff Stuff Magazine • AT5242.................................$18.95
Springfield Armory Shoulder Weapons, 1795-1968 • Robert W. D. Ball • AT5749 ....$34.95

Published by Antique Trader Books

P.O. Box 1050 • Dubuque, IA • 52004-1050 • Credit Card Orders Call 1-800-334-7165
www.collect.com/atbooks
Sales Tax and Shipping and Handling Charges Apply